Business Succession -Control. Alt. Delete. Reset. Copyright © 2023 by Fusion Dynamics and You LLC All rights reserved.

No part of this workbook may be used or reproduced in any manner whatsoever without written permission except in the case of reprints in the context of reviews.

Published by Fusion Dynamics and You LLC
www.fdyconsultants.com

ISBN: 978-1-960973-01-6

AF889183

Welcome!

DR. KINDALL BUNDY, MBA, QMHP, CDP

Dr. Kindall Bundy has over 20 years of experience pioneering business practices, significantly enhancing organizations and businesses within the Richmond, Virginia area and its surrounding counties. Throughout his career, he has focused on innovation, research, and the implementation of strategic resources. Building on his expertise, Dr. Bundy founded FD&Y Consultants, a firm dedicated to providing guidance to young individuals, professionals, and businesses. His work emphasizes skill development, forward-thinking business planning, community enhancement, the provision of supportive resources, and effective succession planning. Dr. Bundy is committed to helping organizations and individuals achieve sustainable growth and success through targeted development and strategic planning.

FD&Y CONSULTANTS	2023

Control. Alt. Delete. Reset.

Making the Shift

This toolkit is specifically designed to support CEOs, organizational leaders, career professionals, and entrepreneurs in maximizing their progress and effectiveness. It provides essential resources and strategies to enhance leadership skills, drive organizational success, and foster personal and professional growth. Whether you are leading a company, advancing your career, or growing your own business, this toolkit equips you with the tools necessary to excel and navigate challenges effectively.

Over the next month, you'll explore the difference between being busy and being productive, define a monthly focus aligned with your goals, and gain clarity on actionable steps for success.

You will also find tools to prevent burnout, including the Professional Burnout Worksheet and Burnout Prevention Workbook, helping you embrace intentional leadership and overcome toxic productivity.

Whether you are scaling a business, leading a team, or advancing your career, this toolkit equips you to manage yourself, take aligned action daily, and accelerate meaningful results.

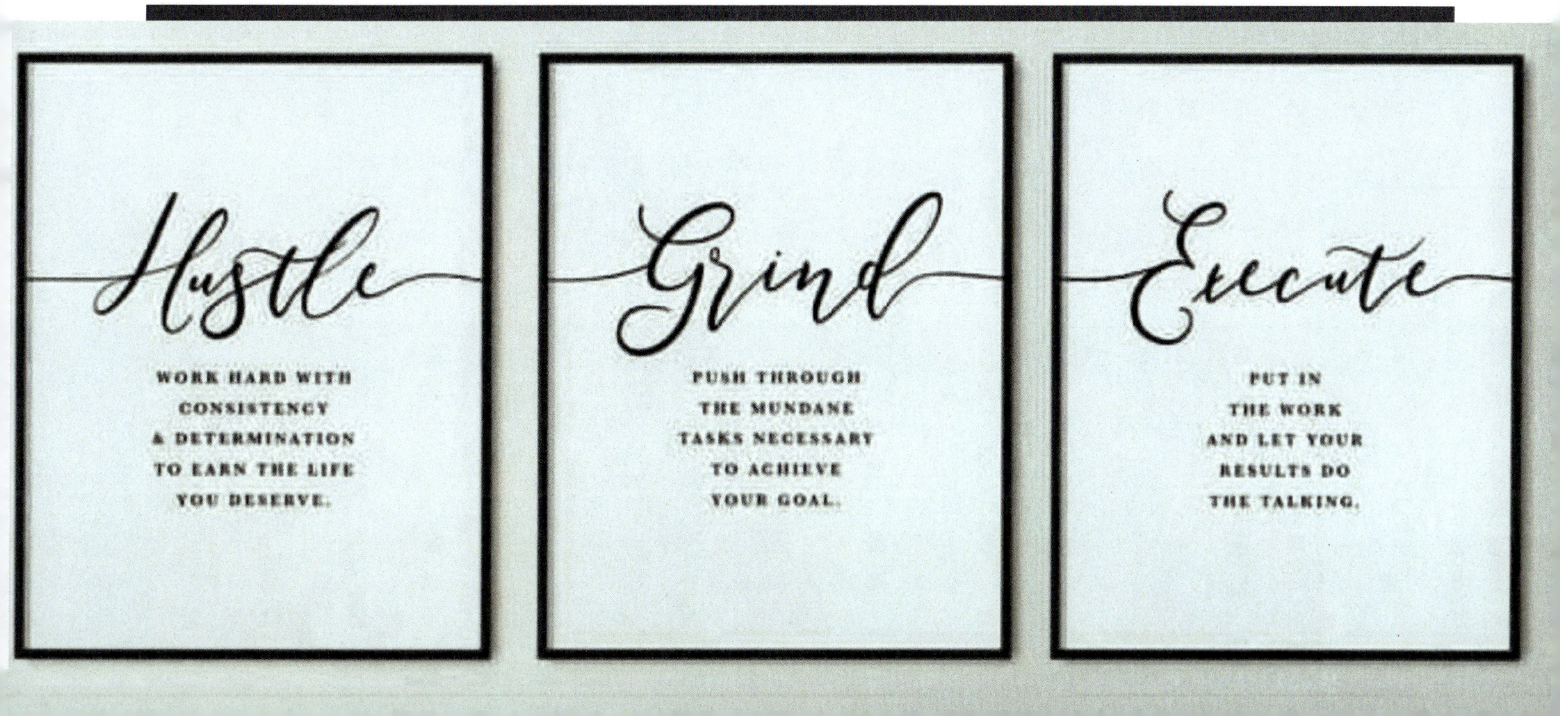

CONTENTS

What's Next?

- Reflect on what you've learned in this toolkit. Identify one chapter or topic that resonated most with you and start implementing those strategies today.
- Stay curious! Continue reading, researching, and learning about personal development. Growth is an ongoing process.
- Share your knowledge. Teaching others what you've learned reinforces your own understanding and creates a ripple effect of self-empowerment.

"Rest is not a reward for doing enough. It is a requirement for becoming whole. True productivity begins with the courage to pause."
— Dr. Kindall Bundy

Final Thoughts:

In a professional environment that often equates busyness with productivity, mindful planning and effective time management are critical for senior executives committed to living intentionally. This chapter will guide you through strategies for purposeful planning, helping you manage your time in alignment with your values and goals. Central to this process is integrating rest and reflection into your routine, a practice that allows you to recalibrate, gain clarity, and make informed decisions.

Using the Bundy Model—Control, Alt, Delete, and Reset—you will learn to take charge of your time and energy, shift perspectives, eliminate distractions, and periodically reassess your approach to ensure continued growth and alignment with your objectives.

- **Control:** Take deliberate control of your schedule by setting boundaries and prioritizing time for both work and rest. Recognizing when to step back and recharge is crucial for maintaining long-term productivity.

- **Alt:** Shift your approach to time management by embracing intentional planning. Adjust your perspective to focus on quality over quantity, ensuring that each decision and action aligns with your strategic goals.

- **Delete:** Eliminate unnecessary tasks and distractions that don't serve your purpose, creating space for what truly matters. This includes saying no to non-essential commitments that may interfere with your ability to rest and reflect.

- **Reset:** Regularly reset your intentions and plans to stay adaptable. Building in moments of rest and reflection allows you to recalibrate and ensure your actions remain aligned with your evolving goals and values.

The journey toward intentionality is personal and ongoing. It's about finding balance, purpose, and fulfillment in a way that resonates with your unique values and aspirations. Integrating rest and reflection into your life, along with a commitment to adapt and evolve, establishes a sustainable practice of intentional living. Keep moving forward, one intentional step at a time, knowing that each decision you make brings you closer to the leadership and life you envision.

Best Wishes,

Dr. Kindall M. Bundy

References

B.
Baumeister, R. F., & Tierney, J. (2011). *Willpower: Rediscovering the greatest human strength*. Penguin Press.
Brown, B. (2010). *The gifts of imperfection: Let go of who you think you're supposed to be and embrace who you are*. Hazelden.

C.
Clear, J. (2018). *Atomic habits: An easy & proven way to build good habits & break bad ones*. Avery.
Cloud, H., & Townsend, J. (1992). *Boundaries: When to say yes, how to say no to take control of your life*. Zondervan.

D.
Duhigg, C. (2012). *The power of habit: Why we do what we do in life and business*. Random House.

M.
Maslach, C., & Leiter, M. P. (2016). *Burnout: The cost of caring*. Malor Books.
Maslach, C., & Leiter, M. P. (2017). *The truth about burnout: How organizations cause personal stress and what to do about it*. Jossey-Bass.

N.
Naparstek, B. (2004). *Invisible heroes: Survivors of trauma and how they heal*. Bantam.
Neff, K. (2011). *Self-compassion: The proven power of being kind to yourself*. William Morrow.
Newport, C. (2016). *Deep work: Rules for focused success in a distracted world*. Grand Central Publishing.

P.
Pang, A. S. (2016). *Rest: Why you get more done when you work less*. Basic Books.
Peters, T. (2019). *The burnout fix: Overcome overwhelm, beat busy, and sustain success in the new world of work*. Wiley.

S.
Smith, C. (2017). *Make it happen: Surrender your fear. Take the leap. Live on purpose.* Thomas Nelson.

Made in United States
Orlando, FL
06 November 2026

90241459R00074

CONTROL, ALT, DELETE, AND RESET

- THE MODEL
- THE ROLE OF LEADERSHIP (BUSY VS. PRODUCTIVE)
- THE POWER OF AUTHENTICITY
- AUTHENTICITY AND THE BUNDY MODEL OF LEADERSHIP

CH.1

The Model

In the context of the Bundy Model, "Control, Alt, Delete, and Reset" serve as essential tools for leaders and corporations to effectively manage change, improve processes, and reset their focus toward future success. Each component represents a core principle that guides both personal and organizational transformation, promoting adaptability, accountability, and strategic decision-making. Here's an in-depth explanation of what a leader and corporation need for success in relation to each concept:

Control

Meaning: Control refers to taking proactive ownership of one's environment, mindset, and actions. For a leader or corporation, it means effectively managing all factors within their sphere of influence, ensuring that resources, time, and energy are directed toward achieving the organization's objectives. This concept emphasizes accountability, decisiveness, and focus in leadership and business operations.

Extensive Meaning:

- **Leadership Context:** Leaders must control their vision, strategy, and team dynamics. This involves making informed, strategic decisions that align with the organization's long-term goals while maintaining clarity and focus in execution. Effective control means balancing the operational, financial, and human aspects of leadership to drive success and sustain performance. Leaders should empower their teams, setting clear expectations and ensuring each member is aligned with the overall mission.
- **Corporate Context:** In a corporate setting, control involves managing internal processes, maintaining consistent communication, and ensuring resources are being used efficiently. It requires the ability to make adjustments and course corrections in real-time, responding to both internal and external changes. Control also includes managing the culture, as leadership's mindset can influence organizational values, morale, and direction.

For success, leaders and corporations must understand the importance of maintaining control of their operations, cultivating a growth mindset, and holding themselves and others accountable for results. Strategic planning and an agile approach to decision-making allow organizations to stay on track in the face of external challenges and opportunities.

Alt (Alternative)

Meaning: The "Alt" in the Bundy Model encourages exploring alternative solutions, strategies, and approaches. It stresses the importance of adaptability and innovation in both leadership and organizational practices. Leaders must embrace the concept of flexibility, constantly reassessing and adapting their strategies as necessary to stay ahead of industry trends, market demands, and evolving challenges.

Extensive Meaning:

- **Leadership Context:** A successful leader is one who not only reacts to problems but also anticipates them by considering alternative strategies and creative solutions. By fostering a culture of innovation and risk-taking, leaders create environments where new ideas are welcomed and tested. Alternative approaches allow leaders to pivot quickly, ensuring the organization stays competitive and responsive.
- **Corporate Context:** Corporations that embrace alternatives are better positioned to identify opportunities, streamline processes, and explore new business models. Being willing to pivot and adjust to changing market conditions is key to staying relevant. Alternative strategies can lead to more efficient processes, cost reductions, or more effective customer solutions.

For success, leaders must encourage a culture of creativity and flexibility, ensuring the organization is prepared to adjust quickly and embrace change when necessary.

Delete

Meaning: "Delete" involves eliminating outdated, inefficient, or counterproductive practices, beliefs, or systems. It's about shedding what no longer adds value to the organization or individual. For a leader and corporation to succeed, they need to constantly evaluate and refine their practices, removing anything that hinders growth or progress.

Extensive Meaning:

- **Leadership Context:** Leaders must have the foresight and courage to recognize when certain strategies, processes, or mindsets are no longer effective. This could include ending underperforming projects, cutting unnecessary costs, or eliminating poor-performing teams or practices. The ability to delete inefficiencies fosters a leaner, more agile leadership approach.
- **Corporate Context:** Corporations need to routinely evaluate their operations, products, and services to determine what's no longer serving the company's objectives. This can mean updating outdated technologies, restructuring departments, or even reassessing customer feedback. Constantly pruning what isn't working enables organizations to focus on what drives value and supports future growth.

For success, both leaders and corporations must be willing to let go of inefficiencies, embrace ongoing improvement, and remove what no longer serves the organization's goals.

Reset

Meaning: "Reset" signifies the need for reflection and realignment of priorities, goals, and strategies. Leaders and corporations must occasionally take a step back, assess their current situation, and reset their trajectory in alignment with evolving goals, values, or market conditions.

Extensive Meaning:

- **Leadership Context:** Successful leaders understand that to remain effective, they must periodically reset their focus—reassessing their mission, vision, and goals. This reset often comes after a significant shift, such as a market change, leadership transition, or organizational restructuring. It ensures that leaders and teams remain aligned and motivated, with clear objectives moving forward.
- **Corporate Context:** Corporations must periodically engage in strategic planning sessions or audits to reset their business strategies, review progress toward long-term goals, and ensure that resources are effectively allocated. This reset could involve changing business models, refreshing branding efforts, or launching new initiatives to meet changing customer needs.

For success, organizations must embrace the concept of periodic reflection and strategic realignment, ensuring that their efforts remain aligned with both internal aspirations and external market conditions.

In summary, the Bundy Model's "Control, Alt, Delete, and Reset" provides a framework for leaders and corporations to thrive in an ever-changing business environment. Leaders must control their strategies and actions, be open to alternative solutions and innovation, delete inefficiencies and outdated practices, and reset their goals to stay aligned with the organization's vision. This holistic approach enables businesses to adapt, grow, and succeed by fostering a dynamic and accountable leadership culture, ensuring long-term sustainability and growth.

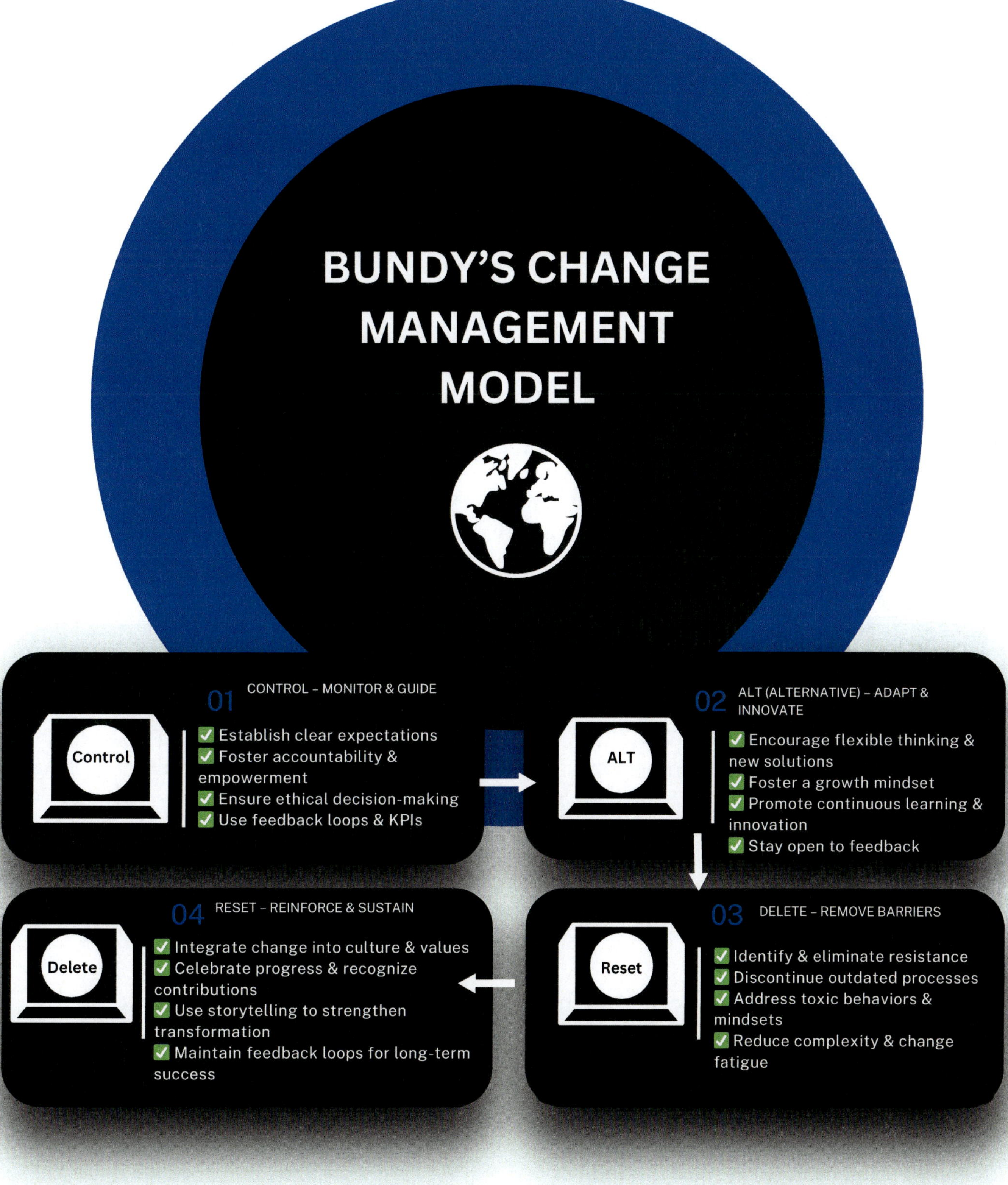
BUNDY'S CHANGE MANAGEMENT MODEL
01 CONTROL – MONITOR & GUIDE
Control
✅ Establish clear expectations
✅ Foster accountability & empowerment
✅ Ensure ethical decision-making
✅ Use feedback loops & KPIs
02 ALT (ALTERNATIVE) – ADAPT & INNOVATE
ALT
✅ Encourage flexible thinking & new solutions
✅ Foster a growth mindset
✅ Promote continuous learning & innovation
✅ Stay open to feedback
03 DELETE – REMOVE BARRIERS
Reset
✅ Identify & eliminate resistance
✅ Discontinue outdated processes
✅ Address toxic behaviors & mindsets
✅ Reduce complexity & change fatigue
04 RESET – REINFORCE & SUSTAIN
Delete
✅ Integrate change into culture & values
✅ Celebrate progress & recognize contributions
✅ Use storytelling to strengthen transformation
✅ Maintain feedback loops for long-term success

In the context of leadership, being busy versus being productive can significantly impact a leader's ability to manage their strategies, adapt to alternative solutions, remove inefficiencies, and realign their goals to stay focused on the organization's vision. Here's a breakdown of how these concepts relate to the key aspects of the Bundy Model:

Being Busy vs. Being Productive

1. **Being Busy:**

Being busy refers to being engaged in a high volume of tasks, activities, or operations, often without assessing whether these efforts are aligned with strategic goals or driving meaningful progress. Leaders may feel like they're accomplishing a lot, but their actions may not be focused on the most impactful outcomes. They might be caught up in day-to-day operations, firefighting, or responding to every immediate issue, leading to a cycle of constant activity without delivering long-term value.

In the Bundy Model context:

- **Control:** Leaders who are busy may focus on micromanaging small tasks and responding to every demand, rather than steering the company with a clear vision and strategy. They may be controlling every minor detail, which can lead to burnout or inefficiency.
- **Alt (Alternative):** Being busy can prevent leaders from exploring alternative approaches or innovative solutions, as they are too absorbed in existing processes or stuck in routines.
- **Delete:** Busy leaders may struggle to identify outdated practices or inefficiencies, as they are focused on maintaining the current workload rather than reassessing what's not working.
- **Reset:** Busyness can prevent leaders from taking time to reset and reflect on the bigger picture or long-term goals, as they are consumed with immediate tasks that don't contribute to future success.

2. **Being Productive:**

Being productive is about focusing on high-priority tasks that directly contribute to achieving the organization's objectives, growth, and long-term vision. It's not about doing more things; it's about doing the right things that create value, drive progress, and align with strategic goals. Productive leaders work smarter, not harder, by focusing on tasks that move the organization forward, using resources efficiently, and prioritizing actions that have the most significant impact.

In the Bundy Model context:

- **Control:** Productive leaders maintain control over their time and resources, ensuring that their efforts are aligned with strategic goals. They delegate effectively, focus on high-impact initiatives, and manage their environment and mindset to achieve long-term success.
- **Alt (Alternative):** Productive leaders actively seek alternative solutions, embrace innovation, and foster creativity within their teams to solve problems and improve processes. They are not locked into old ways of doing things but are continuously evolving.
- **Delete:** Productive leaders regularly assess and eliminate outdated practices, inefficiencies, or distractions that hinder progress. They create streamlined processes and focus on value-driven activities.
- **Reset:** Productive leaders make time for reflection, periodically resetting their strategies and goals to ensure they remain aligned with the organization's vision. They continuously assess performance and adapt to changing circumstances.

Key Differences Between Being Busy and Being Productive in Leadership

- **Efficiency vs. Effectiveness:**

Being busy often leads to inefficiency, where a leader expends energy on tasks that don't contribute to larger goals. Being productive, on the other hand, is about being effective—prioritizing actions that drive outcomes that are aligned with the organization's mission and vision.

- **Focus on Long-Term vs. Short-Term:**

Leaders who are busy tend to focus on short-term, reactive tasks. Productive leaders, however, balance their focus between immediate needs and long-term strategy, ensuring their efforts are aligned with the company's broader objectives.

- **Strategic Alignment:**

Busy leaders may lose sight of the bigger picture because they are entrenched in day-to-day operations. Productive leaders consistently reassess their actions to ensure alignment with the company's vision and adjust strategies as needed.

- **Innovation vs. Routine:**

Busyness often leads to a focus on routine tasks and a resistance to change, while productivity encourages innovation and a willingness to explore new, alternative approaches to improve processes and drive progress.

In the context of the Bundy Model, the key to being a productive leader is the ability to control one's actions strategically, while also being open to alternative solutions and innovation, consistently deleting inefficiencies, and regularly resetting goals to stay aligned with the organization's vision. Being busy, on the other hand, often leads to burnout and a lack of strategic focus, limiting the leader's ability to drive meaningful change or progress. Successful leaders prioritize productivity over busyness, ensuring that their efforts directly contribute to organizational success and long-term growth.

Busy vs. Productive

The hard working leader that is always busy but never makes money...	The mindful leader that manages their time strategically and makes a great return on their time invested...	Forward- Thinking Solution
Has many priorities	Has only a few priorities	Revisit your WHY & write down daily, weekly & monthly priorities
Confuses requests and shiny objects with opportunities and says YES often	Knows when to say NO: Whenever something isn't aligned with his/her priorities	Use the affirmations from the self-management worksheet daily before checking social media or email
Mulittasks	Does one task at a time	Set a 30 minute reminder on your phone to close all tabs except the ones you need to get your current task done
Gets lost in details	Focuses on the big picture	Use this 50k roadmap to create a roadmap for yourself. Place it somewhere, where you can clearly see it when working.

Busy vs. Productive

The hard working leader that is always busy but never makes money...	The mindful leader that manages their time strategically and makes a great return on their time invested...	Solution
Takes on all the responsibilities	Eliminates or delegates tasks	Work on past wounds to identify what benefit you have from taking on all responsibilities so that you can be more mindful about that in the future. Use the affirmations from the self-management worksheet. Use the Eisenhower priority matrix from the self-management worksheet to identify tasks to elminiminate or delegate.
Has no schedule or a fully packed schedule	Allocates time for reflection and planning. Has realistic timelines for small task and big goals.	Use calendar blocking to schedule your days and the to dos you committed to in your self-management worksheet.
Always on their phone and easily distracted	Close doors on all distractions	Give yourself phone times. Close your tabs. Stick to scheduled times and tasks. Track how long it takes to complete 1 task.

Busy vs. Productive

The hard working leader that is always busy but never makes money...	The mindful leader that manages their time strategically and makes a great return on their time invested...	Solution
Always in creation (course materials, a new product, homepage, random social media content, branding...) and never in selling mode	Always sells first and then creates	Use this presell checklist and start preselling your offers
Self sabotages because of fear of short term losses, a lack of a long term strategy and understanding of numbers and target KPIs	Has a bigger understanding of their numbers and is happy to spend money today to acquire a customer and create opportunities that are worth more tomorrow	Understand Acquisition Cost VS Customer Lifetime Value The ideal CAC to CLV Ratio is 3:1 - if over the lifetime of a customer you can expect to earn 1k you can spend 333$ to acquire this customer

Leader Productivity Worksheet

Applying the Bundy Model (Control, Alt, Delete, and Reset)

This worksheet will help you assess your leadership approach and identify ways to improve productivity using the Bundy Model's four key concepts: Control, Alt, Delete, and Reset. Reflect on each section and answer the questions provided. Use this as a guide to enhance your effectiveness and ensure that your actions align with both short-term and long-term goals.

1. Control: Taking Charge of Your Environment, Mindset, and Actions

Objective: Assess how well you manage your actions, decisions, and the environment around you. Are you focused on the right goals? Are you accountable for your outcomes?

- How do you manage your time and resources?

e.g., Do you prioritize high-impact tasks? Do you delegate effectively?

- Are you clear about your role and the organization's goals?

e.g., How well do you understand the organization's vision, and how do your actions align with that vision?

- How do you hold yourself and your team accountable?

e.g., Do you track progress on key projects and goals? Do you provide feedback and guidance regularly?

- What strategies do you use to stay focused?

e.g., How do you avoid distractions and stay aligned with your priorities?

Action Steps:

- List 1-2 areas where you could improve your focus and control:

2. Alt (Alternative): Embracing Innovation and Flexibility

Objective: Reflect on your openness to exploring new solutions and adapting to changing circumstances.

- How do you encourage creative thinking and problem-solving in your team?

e.g., Do you foster an environment that supports new ideas and innovation?

- Are you open to exploring alternative solutions when facing obstacles?

e.g., How often do you challenge the status quo or seek better ways of doing things?

- How do you respond to changes or disruptions in the workplace?

e.g., Do you stay flexible, and how do you manage change effectively?

- Are you willing to experiment and take calculated risks?

e.g., Do you support initiatives that may involve uncertainty or innovation?

Action Steps:

- Identify one area where you can introduce more innovation or flexibility:

3. **Delete:** Removing Inefficiencies and Outdated Practices

Objective: Evaluate the areas where you and your organization can eliminate inefficiencies, redundant processes, or outdated strategies that no longer serve the overall mission.

- What outdated practices or processes do you still rely on?

e.g., Are there old ways of working that hinder progress or use up valuable resources?

- How do you assess and improve team or organizational performance?

e.g., Do you regularly evaluate what's working and what's not?

- Do you have any habits or routines that are not contributing to your growth or productivity?

e.g., Are there personal habits you need to reassess or eliminate to become more productive?

- What processes or structures could be streamlined for better efficiency?

e.g., Are there bottlenecks or inefficiencies in your operations that you need to address?

Action Steps:

- Identify one inefficiency or outdated practice to eliminate:

4. **Reset: Reassessing and Realigning Goals**

Objective: Reflect on how often you reset your priorities and ensure that your actions and goals remain aligned with the organization's overall vision.

- When was the last time you evaluated your leadership goals and personal growth?

e.g., How often do you reflect on where you are and where you want to go?

- How do you realign your strategies if they're not producing the desired results?

e.g., What do you do when things are not going according to plan? Do you course-correct effectively?

- Are you regularly assessing the organization's vision and adjusting your approach?

e.g., How do you ensure your team and business remain aligned with long-term goals?

- What steps do you take to reset after setbacks or challenges?

e.g., How do you recover and refocus after difficult periods?

Action Steps:

- Define one personal or organizational goal you want to reset or realign:

Final Reflection and Action Plan

- Based on your answers, what is the most important area you need to focus on right now (Control, Alt, Delete, or Reset)?

- What are 2-3 actionable steps you can take in the next month to improve in that area?

a. ____

b. ____

c. ____

- How will you measure progress in these areas?

This worksheet is designed to help you evaluate and improve your leadership effectiveness by reflecting on how well you implement the principles of the Bundy Model. By focusing on Control, Alt, Delete, and Reset, you can become a more productive leader who drives meaningful change and aligns with your organization's vision.

The Power of Authenticity

The concept of "Power" in authentic leadership refers to the influence a leader has over others, stemming from their genuine self-awareness, transparency, and ethical conduct. In the context of authentic leadership, power is not about coercion or control but about inspiring trust, commitment, and respect. The power comes from a leader's ability to connect with others on a deeper, more meaningful level by remaining true to their core values, building credibility, and creating an environment of openness and empowerment.

Why is this power important?

1. Trust and Credibility: Authentic leaders build strong, trusting relationships with their teams. This trust becomes a form of power that encourages collaboration, creativity, and loyalty. When employees trust their leader, they are more likely to be engaged and motivated.
2. Emotional Impact: The ability to connect with others emotionally is a powerful tool in leadership. By demonstrating vulnerability, empathy, and openness, an authentic leader can foster a culture of psychological safety where people feel valued and respected.
3. Inspiration and Influence: Authentic leaders are often viewed as role models. Their power stems from their ability to inspire others to act with integrity and purpose. This kind of influence is long-lasting and rooted in shared values rather than short-term manipulation.

Why is it important to identify one's leadership style?

1. Self-awareness: Knowing your leadership style helps you understand your strengths and areas for growth. Authentic leadership requires a high level of self-awareness to ensure that actions and decisions align with your core values and beliefs.
2. Consistency and Authenticity: Understanding your style allows you to lead consistently and authentically, which is essential for maintaining trust. If your actions align with your leadership style, others are more likely to see you as genuine and reliable.
3. Effective Communication: Different leadership styles require different approaches to communication. By identifying your style, you can adapt your communication to be more effective with different individuals and teams.
4. Enhanced Relationships: Recognizing your leadership style helps you build better relationships with others by understanding how they perceive you and how you can best support them. It also enables you to navigate conflicts and challenges in a way that is true to your values.
5. Adaptability: Leaders may encounter different situations that require different approaches. Knowing your style can help you adjust and adapt when necessary, ensuring you're flexible without losing sight of your core principles.

In summary, the power of authentic leadership lies in the ability to influence others in a positive, ethical way. Identifying one's leadership style is key to cultivating that power, ensuring alignment with personal values, and creating an environment where others can thrive.

Authenticity and the Bundy Model of Leadership

The Bundy Model of Control, Alt. Delete, and Reset is a metaphorical framework that can be very helpful in enhancing authentic leadership and promoting leaders into leadership roles. By using the concepts of "Control," "Alt," "Delete," and "Reset," leaders can engage in continuous self-reflection, growth, and transformation, all of which are essential to authentic leadership. Let's break down each element of the model and see how it applies to authentic leadership:

1. **Control (Self-awareness and Accountability)**
   - What it means: In the Bundy model, "Control" is about taking charge of your thoughts, actions, and decisions. For authentic leaders, this means having a deep self-awareness and understanding of your values, strengths, and weaknesses. A leader who can control their emotions, responses, and decisions is seen as steady, reliable, and trustworthy.
   - **How it enhances authentic leadership:**
     - Self-regulation: Authentic leaders must maintain control over their emotions and reactions, especially in challenging situations. This helps them lead with integrity and model calmness for their teams.
     - Accountability: By controlling their actions and being accountable for both successes and failures, leaders build credibility and trust. They lead by example and encourage the same behavior in others.
   - **How it promotes leadership roles:** A leader who shows control in high-pressure situations will naturally attract followers who respect their composure and decision-making ability. This sense of trustworthiness is critical for moving into leadership positions.
2. **Alt. (Adaptation and Flexibility)**
   - **What it means:** The "Alt" function in the model represents adaptation or the ability to adjust when faced with new or changing circumstances. An Authentic leader is not rigid or one-dimensional; they understand that leadership often requires different approaches depending on the situation or people involved.
   - **How it enhances authentic leadership:**
     - Flexibility: Authentic leaders must be flexible enough to alter their approach as needed, while still staying true to their core values. They adapt their leadership style based on the needs of their team and the situation.

  - Growth mindset: Adaptation also includes learning and evolving. Authentic leaders are open to feedback, willing to learn from mistakes, and continuously strive for improvement.
- **How it promotes leadership roles:** Being adaptable is crucial for leaders to deal with the ever-changing challenges in organizations. Leaders who can adjust without losing sight of their principles are often seen as forward-thinking and capable of guiding teams through transitions.

3. **Delete (Letting Go of Ineffective Practices)**

- What it means: "Delete" represents the need to remove ineffective practices, toxic behaviors, or outdated thinking. In authentic leadership, this means letting go of old habits, biases, or approaches that no longer serve the team or organization. Authentic leaders have the courage to make tough decisions, such as eliminating practices that harm productivity, morale, or organizational culture.
- **How it enhances authentic leadership:**
  - Self-reflection: By "deleting" ineffective behaviors or ways of thinking, leaders reflect on how they can grow and evolve. Authentic leaders must be willing to rid themselves of negative traits like arrogance, defensiveness, or micromanagement.
  - Prioritizing values: Leaders who let go of toxic practices can align their actions more closely with their personal and organizational values, thus fostering an environment of transparency, trust, and respect.
- **How it promotes leadership roles**: Leaders who are willing to eliminate outdated or counterproductive practices can foster an environment of continuous improvement, innovation, and respect. This openness to change positions them as leaders who can guide organizations toward progress.

4. **Reset (Reinvention and Renewal)**

- What it means: "Reset" involves reassessing and reorienting oneself toward new goals or strategies. Authentic leaders periodically need to "reset" their mindset, priorities, and approach to reflect on what is working and what needs to change. A reset is a deliberate act of starting fresh, learning from past experiences, and creating new directions for growth.
- **How it enhances authentic leadership:**
  - **Renewed perspective:** By taking time to reset, leaders can step back, reassess their strategies, and ensure their leadership remains aligned with their core values. This moment of renewal allows for reinvigorated energy and vision.
  - **Encouraging innovation:** Resetting also opens the door to creativity and new solutions. Leaders who embrace the idea of constantly resetting their goals can inspire innovation within their teams.
- **How it promotes leadership roles:** Authentic leaders who are able to reset will be seen as adaptable, visionary, and resilient. Their willingness to embrace change and start anew when needed sets them apart as effective leaders who can guide teams and organizations through evolving challenges.

In Summary:
The Bundy Model of Control, Alt, Delete, and Reset offers a systematic approach to improving and enhancing authentic leadership.

- **Control** allows leaders to maintain self-awareness and accountability.
- **Alt** represents flexibility and the ability to adapt to new circumstances.
- **Delete** signifies letting go of outdated practices or behaviors that hinder growth.
- **Reset** offers an opportunity for reinvention and renewed purpose.

By continuously engaging with these principles, authentic leaders can remain grounded in their core values, while also evolving and growing in response to new challenges. This cycle of reflection, adaptation, and renewal not only helps them become more effective leaders but also prepares them to take on new leadership roles with a solid foundation of trust and integrity.

CHANGE MANAGEMENT

- UNDERSTANDING CHANGE MANAGEMENT
- WHY IS CHANGE MANAGEMENT IMPORTANT FOR SUCCESSION PLANNING?
- WHY DOES LEADERSHIP MATTER, AND WHO IS AFFECTED IF BAD LEADERSHIP IS OBTAINED?
- WHAT IS THE COMPENSATION FOR A 2025 LEADER OF A FORTUNE 500, GOVERNMENT LEADERSHIP ROLE, AND FORTUNE 1000?
- HOW DOES THE "RIGHT" LEADER FIND THE JOB?
- RESUME BUILDING FOR AN AUTHENTIC LEADER BASED ON THE BUNDY MODEL

CH.2

Understanding Change Management: What is it?

Change management refers to the process, tools, and techniques used to manage the people-side of change in an organization. It involves preparing, supporting, and helping individuals and teams in the organization to adapt to changes that occur, whether they are related to processes, technology, structure, or culture. Change management ensures that changes are implemented smoothly, minimizing disruptions while maximizing engagement and adoption.

Why is Change Management Important for Succession Planning?

Succession planning is the process of identifying and developing new leaders to take over key positions when they become vacant. Effective change management plays a vital role in succession planning because:

1. **Smooth Transitions:** It helps organizations manage leadership transitions smoothly, ensuring that leadership roles are filled with qualified candidates who can maintain continuity.
2. **Preparedness:** Change management practices ensure that future leaders are well-prepared to handle organizational changes by equipping them with the necessary skills and mindset to manage change.
3. **Talent Development**: It allows organizations to identify high-potential individuals and nurture them to take on more significant roles in the future, reducing leadership gaps when key individuals leave.
4. **Cultural Continuity:** As organizations evolve, change management helps maintain and adapt the organizational culture, aligning future leaders with the company's values and objectives.

Why Does Leadership Matter, and Who is Affected If Bad Leadership is Obtained?

Leadership matters because effective leaders set the tone for the organization, driving culture, productivity, and strategy. They influence decisions, employee engagement, innovation, and the organization's overall success. Bad leadership can have wide-reaching consequences, including:

- **Employee Morale:** Poor leadership can lead to low morale, disengagement, and high turnover among employees, which negatively impacts productivity.

- **Organizational Performance:** Ineffective leaders often struggle to make timely and strategic decisions, which can hinder the organization's ability to stay competitive and respond to challenges.

- **Reputation and Trust:** Bad leadership can erode trust both internally (among employees) and externally (with clients, customers, and stakeholders), damaging the company's reputation.

- **Culture and Values:** Leadership shapes an organization's culture. Bad leadership can lead to toxic work environments, poor communication, and misalignment of values.

Who is affected?

- **Employees:** They are often the most directly impacted by bad leadership through poor work conditions, stress, lack of clarity, and limited opportunities for growth.
- **Customers:** Inconsistent leadership can affect product or service quality, customer relationships, and brand trust.
- **Stakeholders and Shareholders:** Bad leadership can lead to financial underperformance, mismanagement of resources, and loss of shareholder value.
- **The Organization as a Whole:** When leadership fails, the entire organization may struggle to meet goals, execute strategy, and innovate effectively.

What is the Compensation for a 2025 Leader of a Fortune 500, Government Leadership Role, and Fortune 1000?

Compensation packages for leaders at these levels vary greatly depending on the organization, the region, and the industry. However, general compensation trends for 2025 could be as follows:

- **Fortune 500 CEO:**
  - Base Salary: $1.5 million - $2.5 million annually.
  - Bonus and Incentives: Can range from 50% to 200% of base salary, depending on company performance.
  - Stock Options/Equity: Often a significant portion of the compensation, potentially millions, aligned with the company's long-term success.
  - Total Compensation: Total compensation packages for a CEO of a Fortune 500 company can reach $20 million to $50 million per year or more, depending on performance bonuses, stock options, and other perks.

- **Government Leadership Role (e.g., U.S. Federal Government):**
  - Base Salary: U.S. federal government leaders (e.g., Cabinet members or agency heads) typically earn between $200,000 and $250,000 annually.
  - Perks and Benefits: These roles may include additional allowances for security, travel, and housing (depending on position).
  - Total Compensation: While the base salary is lower than in the private sector, government leaders often benefit from job stability, prestige, and post-office pension plans, which can offer substantial long-term compensation.

- **Fortune 1000 CEO/Executive Leader:**
  - Base Salary: $900,000 - $1.5 million annually.
  - Bonus and Incentives: These can range from 30% to 150% of base salary.
  - Stock Options/Equity: Executives in Fortune 1000 companies may receive significant stock options or long-term incentive compensation, sometimes reaching several million dollars.
  - Total Compensation: Compensation can range from $10 million to $30 million annually, depending on company performance, industry, and specific role.

How Does the "Right" Leader Find the Job?

The right leader often finds the job through a combination of personal qualities, networking, and career strategy. Here are some ways that a leader can find the right job:

- **Networking and Relationships:**
  - Connections: Many high-level leadership positions are filled through networking and personal connections. A strong professional network can provide access to executive headhunters and insider job opportunities.
  - Mentorship: Having mentors and advisors who can guide career decisions and introduce them to leadership opportunities is key to advancing into top roles.

- **Demonstrating Leadership Success:**
  - Proven Track Record: Leaders who have demonstrated successful leadership in their current roles, with measurable results, are more likely to be noticed for future leadership roles.
  - Reputation: A leader's personal brand and reputation for being authentic, trustworthy, and capable will help attract opportunities. Publishing thought leadership, speaking at conferences, and being active in industry discussions can raise a leader's profile.

- **Continuous Learning and Development:**
    - Education and Training: Top leaders invest in continuous development through advanced degrees (such as MBAs or executive education) and professional certifications. This signals competence and ambition.
    - Developing Leadership Skills: Effective leaders are always honing their skills in areas like strategic thinking, communication, and adaptability, which enhances their value to organizations.

- **Executive Search Firms and Recruitment:**
    - Headhunters: Executive search firms specialize in finding top leaders for high-level roles. These firms often work with Fortune 500 and Fortune 1000 companies to identify leaders with the right expertise.
    - Targeted Applications: When the right job appears, highly qualified leaders may proactively apply or be headhunted by companies looking for transformational leaders.

- **Cultural and Organizational Fit:**
    - Alignment with Values: The right leader is often one who aligns with the company's culture, mission, and values. A leader who understands the organization's needs and challenges can be a strong contender for leadership roles.

Change management, leadership effectiveness, and compensation are deeply interwoven. Strong leadership is crucial for organizational success, especially during times of transition. While compensation is an important factor, the best leaders find the right job through reputation, continuous learning, and networking, ensuring they are well-positioned to succeed and lead effectively.

Implementing Change Management

Implementing change management with regard to Authenticity and the Bundy Model of Leadership requires a structured approach to ensure that leaders foster an environment where change is not only accepted but embraced, driven by a commitment to authenticity. Here's a step-by-step guide to implementing change management with a focus on these concepts:

1. Align Leadership with Organizational Values

- **Action:** Begin by ensuring that leadership aligns with the organization's core values and that authenticity is central to the leadership framework. Leaders must first identify and communicate their core values to the team.
- **Bundy Model Implementation:** Use the Bundy model's concepts of Control, Alt, Delete, and Reset to guide leaders through the process of self-reflection, adaptation, and reinvention. This ensures they remain authentic in their decisions, approach to change, and communication during transitions.

2. Promote Authenticity as a Core Value in Change

- **Action:** Authenticity should be embedded as a core value in the change process. This means leaders should be transparent, honest, and consistent in their communication. For instance, when communicating change, leaders should acknowledge potential challenges and openly address concerns, fostering trust.
- **Bundy Model Implementation:** Apply the "Control" aspect to help leaders maintain their emotional intelligence and self-awareness during the change. Use the "Alt" to encourage adaptability as leaders may need to adjust to new circumstances. The "Delete" can help leaders shed ineffective practices that hinder the change process, and "Reset" provides a fresh perspective to steer the organization forward.

3. Involve Employees in the Change Process

- **Action:** Engage employees early and consistently in the change process. Involve them in conversations and decision-making, and ensure their feedback is valued. This fosters a sense of ownership and commitment to the change.
- **Bundy Model Implementation:** Leaders should use the "Alt" component to adapt their leadership style to the needs of different team members, ensuring inclusivity and addressing concerns. This also enables the leader to adapt their approach to communication and decision-making in ways that encourage engagement and participation.

4. Create a Feedback Loop for Continuous Improvement

- **Action:** Encourage ongoing dialogue and feedback during the change process. Authentic leaders foster an open environment where feedback is used to adapt and refine strategies. This ensures that any necessary course corrections are made, and the organization is agile in responding to issues.
- **Bundy Model Implementation:** Leaders should embrace the "Reset" aspect to continuously reassess their strategies and modify them as needed. Regular feedback allows leaders to reset the course and improve their approach, maintaining alignment with the organization's values.

Qualities of a Potential Authentic Leader

To qualify as an authentic leader, a potential leader should have the following qualities:

1. **Self-awareness:** They understand their own values, emotions, and behaviors and how these impact others.
2. **Integrity and Transparency:** They are honest, ethical, and transparent in their actions and decisions.
3. **Emotional Intelligence:** They can manage their own emotions and understand others' emotions, especially in times of change.
4. **Vision and Adaptability:** Authentic leaders can envision the future and adapt to changes while staying true to their values.
5. **Empathy and Active Listening:** They listen deeply to their team, ensuring that every voice is heard and valued.
6. **Resilience:** They remain steadfast in the face of challenges and model a growth mindset for others.

Why Skillset is Important for Organizational Success

Authentic leaders are crucial for organizational success because:

1. **Fostering Trust and Loyalty:** They inspire trust in their teams, which is critical for employee engagement and retention.
2. **Improving Morale and Productivity:** When employees believe in their leader's authenticity, morale and productivity tend to rise.
3. **Navigating Change Successfully:** Authentic leaders are particularly effective in managing change because they bring clarity, empathy, and consistency during transitions.
4. **Creating a Culture of Accountability:** Their transparent and accountable leadership style sets a standard for the entire organization.
5. **Encouraging Innovation:** An authentic leader's openness and adaptability foster an environment where innovation can thrive.

Can an Organization Function Without an Authentic Leader?
An organization can technically function without an authentic leader, but it will likely face significant challenges:

- **Lack of Trust and Engagement:** Without an authentic leader, trust may be difficult to establish, leading to disengaged employees who are less motivated and productive.
- **Increased Conflict:** A lack of transparency and emotional intelligence can result in misunderstandings, conflicts, and a toxic work environment.
- **Inconsistent Decision-making:** An absence of authentic leadership may lead to decision-making that feels arbitrary or self-serving, decreasing organizational cohesion and morale.
- **Difficulty in Change:** Without an authentic leader, leading change can become chaotic, as employees may resist change due to a lack of trust and clear direction.

How Many People Does it Take to Compensate for the Lack of an Authentic Leader?
If an organization lacks an authentic leader, it would take several key individuals to compensate for the void:

1. **Multiple Managers and Team Leads:** Without one authentic leader, multiple managers or team leads with strong interpersonal skills, emotional intelligence, and transparency would need to step up to fill the gap.
2. **HR and Culture Champions:** HR professionals and organizational culture champions would need to lead efforts to build trust and alignment within the organization.
3. **Employee Networks:** Informal leaders, mentors, or employee resource groups can provide guidance, support, and accountability, but this would still require a coordinated effort from several individuals to compensate for the lack of authentic leadership.
4. **Change Agents:** Managing change, specific individuals or teams would need to drive the change process. However, without an authentic leader setting the tone, these efforts could lack direction or face significant resistance.

In essence, it's difficult to compensate for the absence of authentic leadership. While a collaborative effort might cover some aspects, the lack of a clear, central figure who embodies authenticity could significantly undermine organizational success, especially during times of change.

Why Does an Authentic Leader Need to Create a Resume or CV?

For an authentic leader, a resume or CV serves as a critical tool for showcasing their leadership style, personal values, and professional experiences. Here's why creating a resume is so important for an authentic leader:

1. **Clarity of Self:** A resume forces the leader to reflect on their journey, competencies, and the unique ways in which they lead. It helps them clearly communicate their personal and professional identity, which is crucial for an authentic leader who seeks to align their actions with their values.
2. **Building Trust:** Just as authentic leaders build trust within their organizations, they must also build trust with potential employers or partners. A well-crafted resume demonstrates transparency and clarity, two key traits of authentic leadership. It provides a snapshot of the leader's past experiences and accomplishments, giving others confidence in their abilities and leadership style.
3. **Career Progression and Opportunities:** For authentic leaders to continue growing, they must be able to communicate their vision and value proposition effectively. A resume is a powerful tool that opens doors to leadership opportunities, enabling the leader to find roles where their authentic leadership can thrive.
4. **Consistency**: A resume ensures that an authentic leader's experiences and accomplishments are consistently presented in a professional format. It aligns the leader's values with their professional achievements, demonstrating that they are not only committed to success but also to leading in an authentic and purposeful way.

An Authentic leader's resume or CV is not just a list of accomplishments, but a reflection of their leadership philosophy, personal values, and ability to drive change with transparency, empathy, and integrity. It provides potential employers with a roadmap to understanding how the leader operates and how their authentic leadership can contribute to organizational success.

Resume Building for an Authentic Leader Based on the Bundy Model

A well-crafted resume or Curriculum Vitae (CV) is a crucial tool for an authentic leader, as it not only showcases their qualifications and experience but also reflects their leadership style and values. Here's an explanation of why each section is important and how it aligns with the concept of authentic leadership:

CV stands for Curriculum Vitae, which is Latin for "course of life." It is a comprehensive document that outlines a person's educational background, work experience, skills, accomplishments, and other qualifications. A CV is typically more detailed than a resume and may include sections such as publications, research projects, or professional affiliations, depending on the field.

Resume is a French word that means "summary." It is a concise document, usually one to two pages long, that highlights a person's most relevant skills, work experience, education, and accomplishments tailored to a specific job position. A resume is more commonly used in the United States and Canada, while a CV is more common in Europe, the UK, and certain other regions.

In short, the key difference is that a CV is more detailed and comprehensive, while a resume is shorter and more focused.

Executive Summary

The Executive Summary provides a snapshot of the leader's professional identity, key achievements, and leadership approach. For an authentic leader, this section is vital because it sets the tone for the entire resume. It's an opportunity to convey their values, leadership philosophy, and how they approach challenges. Authentic leaders prioritize transparency, self-awareness, and accountability, so this section reflects those traits. It gives potential employers a sense of the leader's personal brand and what they stand for. This part is key for creating an emotional connection with the reader and offering a glimpse into how the leader's mindset and actions align with organizational goals.

Key Competencies

The Key Competencies section highlights the essential skills and qualities that an authentic leader brings to the table. For an authentic leader, this section is important because it demonstrates their self-awareness and emotional intelligence, which are core components of authentic leadership. Competencies like emotional intelligence, change management, and strategic visioning show that the leader is not only capable of achieving results but also attuned to the needs and dynamics of the team. This section helps potential employers understand the leader's skill set and how it will contribute to organizational success.

Professional Experience

The Professional Experience section provides a detailed overview of the leader's career history, showcasing how they've applied their leadership competencies in real-world settings. This section is particularly important for an authentic leader because it demonstrates how they've used transparency, self-awareness, and empathy to drive results. Each role described should reflect how the leader has fostered a culture of trust, encouraged innovation, and empowered teams. Additionally, the specific use of the Bundy Model (Control, Alt, Delete, Reset) in this section highlights how the leader navigates organizational challenges and adapts to change. This practical demonstration of their leadership abilities is essential for showing prospective employers how the leader has consistently applied their authentic leadership style in various contexts.

Education

The Education section is important because it shows the leader's commitment to personal and professional growth, which is a hallmark of authentic leadership. An Authentic leader understands the value of continuous learning, and this section demonstrates that they have invested in gaining the necessary knowledge to succeed in leadership roles. For an authentic leader, having an educational background that combines both business acumen (e.g., an MBA) and personal development (e.g., psychology) reflects a balanced approach to leadership, focusing on both strategic decision-making and understanding human behavior. This dual focus supports their ability to lead with empathy, make informed decisions, and connect with their teams.

Certifications & Professional Development

This section reflects the leader's dedication to continual self-improvement and their investment in acquiring the tools necessary to excel in their role. Certifications such as Certified Change Management Professional (CCMP) and Emotional Intelligence Certification underscore an authentic leader's commitment to mastering the key areas of leadership that are critical for organizational success. For an authentic leader, ongoing development in areas like change management and emotional intelligence ensures they are prepared to lead effectively, manage crises, and drive positive organizational change. This section shows that the leader is actively seeking to refine their skills and stay ahead of industry trends, signaling a growth mindset that is essential for long-term leadership success.

Leadership Philosophy

An authentic leader's Leadership Philosophy is the core of their resume. This section is important because it directly conveys the leader's values, principles, and approach to leadership. It's an opportunity for the leader to articulate how they will bring their authentic self to the role, focusing on aspects like integrity, accountability, and empathy. This section shows the leader's deep commitment to fostering a culture of trust and collaboration, which is the foundation of effective leadership. It also highlights how the leader views their role within the organization—not as someone who imposes control, but as someone who guides and empowers others. In an increasingly complex and fast-paced business world, an authentic leadership philosophy is a key differentiator, demonstrating to employers that the leader can lead with integrity, even in challenging times.

References

Lastly, the References section provides credibility and trustworthiness. For an authentic leader, references can serve as testimonials to their leadership style and impact. The inclusion of references who can speak to the leader's transparency, integrity, and ability to inspire others adds weight to the resume. It signals to potential employers that the leader has built a reputation based on strong relationships, open communication, and proven results. Since authentic leadership is deeply rooted in the idea of building trust, having references that can vouch for these qualities reinforces the leader's credibility.

SUCCESSION PLANNING

FUNDAMENTALS AND THE AUTHENTIC LEADER

- WHAT IS SUCCESSION PLANNING?
- THE NEED FOR THE AUTHENTIC LEADER IN ORGANIZATIONS
- VS. TALENT MANAGEMENT: UNDERSTANDING THE DIFFERENCE
- THE ROLE OF THE AUTHENTIC LEADER IN LONG-TERM SUCCESS

CH.3

What is Succession ?

Succession planning is a strategic process that involves identifying critical positions within an organization and developing a talent pipeline to ensure continuity in leadership. This process prepares employees to step into key roles as others retire or transition to different positions. A successor is an individual equipped with the necessary knowledge, skills, and abilities to temporarily fill a vacant position until a permanent replacement is identified. Succession planning plays a vital role in maintaining business continuity and performance, particularly during leadership transitions. Even when an internal successor is not readily available, it helps identify the competencies, training, and skills required in future external candidates. Failing to implement a succession plan for essential roles poses significant risks to the organization, including the loss of mission-critical knowledge, potential disruptions to workflows and processes, and a decline in performance. Furthermore, it could result in substantial financial losses, making it crucial to address both internal and external recruitment strategies, and ensure the development of necessary skills to mitigate these risks.

The risks include:

 Loss of mission-critical knowledge that may never be recovered.
 Naming a successor and identifying competencies to include personal drive, commitment, knowledge, training, or skills needed to perform the job successfully.
   -Address Internal and External Recruiting
 Significant loss of profit and solutions to recover (possible implementations of new resources, strategies, and or leadership changes/ skill development)
 Potential disruptions to workplace processes, workflows, and protocols

.

AUTHENTIC LEADER VS. TALENT MANAGEMENT

The Need for the Authentic Leader in Organizations vs. Talent Management: Understanding the Difference

Authentic leadership and talent management are both important concepts in the world of business and leadership, but they focus on different aspects of organizational success. Here's a breakdown of each and how they differ:

Authentic Leadership:

Authentic leadership is a leadership style that emphasizes transparency, honesty, and integrity. Authentic leaders are true to themselves and their values, and they foster an environment of trust and openness. Key characteristics of authentic leaders include:

- **Self-awareness:** Understanding one's strengths, weaknesses, values, and emotions.
- **Transparency:** Communicating openly and honestly with team members.
- **Relational transparency:** Showing vulnerability and building trust.
- **Ethical behavior:** Aligning actions with strong moral principles.
- **Balanced processing:** Objectively analyzing information and considering multiple perspectives.

Authentic leaders create environments where employees feel valued and empowered, which often leads to higher engagement, satisfaction, and retention.

Talent Management:

Talent management, on the other hand, is a broader organizational process focused on attracting, developing, and retaining high-performing employees. It involves strategies and practices aimed at managing the human capital within a company. Key components of talent management include:

- **Talent acquisition:** Recruiting the right individuals who align with the company's needs and culture.

- **Employee development:** Offering training, coaching, and growth opportunities to enhance skills and career advancement.
- **Performance management:** Setting goals, evaluating progress, and providing feedback to optimize individual and team performance.
- **Succession planning:** Preparing for future leadership and key position transitions to ensure organizational continuity.
- **Retention strategies:** Creating an environment where employees are motivated to stay long-term.

While talent management focuses on the entire lifecycle of employees, it is centered around optimizing the workforce for organizational success.

Key Differences:

1. **Focus:**
    - Authentic leadership focuses on the individual leader's qualities and their impact on the organization's culture.
    - Talent management focuses on the broader organizational strategy of managing employees, from recruitment to development and retention.
2. **Goal:**
    - The goal of authentic leadership is to foster trust, engagement, and ethical behavior.
    - Talent management aims to optimize the performance and retention of the workforce.
3. **Scope:**
    - Authentic leadership is more about the leader's style and approach to guiding the team.
    - Talent management involves a more strategic, organization-wide approach to human resources.
4. **Impact on Employees:**
    - Authentic leaders create a culture of trust and authenticity that empowers employees.
    - Talent management systems focus on optimizing employee potential and aligning their goals with the organization's objectives.

How They Work Together:

In practice, authentic leadership and talent management can complement each other. For example, authentic leaders can play a significant role in successful talent management by fostering an environment that promotes open communication, employee development, and trust. A company with strong talent management practices will benefit from leaders who can authentically engage and inspire their teams, making talent management efforts more effective.

In summary, authentic leadership emphasizes the individual leader's integrity and approach to relationships, while talent management is about strategically managing the organization's talent pool to drive success. Both contribute to building strong, high-performing organizations but from different angles.

Control, Alt, Delete and Reset Implementation

Applying the Control, Alt, Delete, and Reset (Bundy Model) to Authentic Leadership vs. Talent Management is a strategic framework that allows organizations to assess and realign their processes to improve leadership and talent management practices. Let's break it down and then tie it to organizational sustainability and the role of authentic leadership in Fortune 500, Fortune 1000, and government organizations, along with the impact of the DOGE (2025) government program on change management.

Control, Alt, Delete, and Reset (Bundy Model) Applied to Authentic Leadership vs. Talent Management

- **Control:**
    - **Authentic Leadership:** In an organization, authentic leadership is all about exercising control in a way that is aligned with personal integrity, values, and transparency. Authentic leaders control how they interact with employees, make decisions, and handle crises, ensuring that their actions are consistent with their beliefs. Authentic leaders set the tone for a culture of openness and inclusivity, helping to control the overall workplace environment.
    - **Talent Management:** The control aspect of talent management refers to how organizations manage their human resources. This involves controlling recruitment, employee development programs, performance assessments, and retention strategies. A well-controlled talent management system ensures that the right talent is recruited, developed, and retained in alignment with organizational goals.

- **Alt (Alternative Actions or Perspectives):**
    - **Authentic Leadership:** An authentic leader often encourages alternative perspectives and values feedback. They empower their teams to question the status quo, promote innovation, and suggest alternatives to traditional ways of doing things. By embracing diverse perspectives, authentic leaders create an environment where everyone feels valued and engaged.
    - **Talent Management:** In talent management, the “Alt” component can be seen in how organizations approach employee development. This includes providing opportunities for learning, skill enhancement, and creating career paths that allow employees to explore alternative roles or responsibilities within the organization. It involves fostering an inclusive culture where employees can contribute new ideas and suggest improvements.

- **Delete:**
  - **Authentic Leadership:** The "Delete" step can apply to letting go of outdated leadership practices, biases, and behaviors that undermine trust or hinder employee engagement. An Authentic leader will regularly assess their leadership style and make necessary adjustments to ensure that their approach remains ethical, transparent, and aligned with organizational values.
  - **Talent Management:** For talent management, deleting can refer to eliminating ineffective or outdated talent management practices, such as poorly executed performance reviews or outdated recruitment strategies. Organizations need to regularly assess and update their talent management processes to remain competitive in the market and ensure they are attracting and developing the right talent.
- **Reset:**
  - **Authentic Leadership:** Resetting in the context of authentic leadership means regularly revisiting one's leadership practices, values, and goals to ensure alignment with the organization's evolving needs. An Authentic leader resets their leadership approach after significant changes or feedback, ensuring that they remain in tune with their team's needs and expectations.
  - **Talent Management:** In talent management, resetting involves reevaluating how the organization attracts, develops, and retains talent. This could mean reassessing recruitment channels, learning and development programs, or performance evaluation metrics. Resetting helps ensure the organization's talent strategy is continuously evolving to meet new challenges and objectives.

How Authentic Leadership Contributes to Organizational Sustainability

Authentic leadership plays a critical role in creating an environment where sustainability can thrive. Here's how an authentic leader drives sustainability in an organization:

1. **Fostering Trust and Engagement:** Authentic leaders build strong relationships
2. with their teams based on trust, transparency, and honesty. This trust leads to higher employee engagement, which in turn improves retention, productivity, and long-term sustainability.
3. **Empowering Employees:** Authentic leaders empower employees to contribute meaningfully to the organization's success. This empowerment leads to a more innovative workforce that can adapt and respond to challenges quickly, ensuring long-term viability.
4. **Creating a Culture of Ethical Responsibility:** Authentic leaders emphasize ethical decision-making and lead by example. By doing so, they foster a culture of corporate social responsibility, which contributes to sustainable business practices both internally and externally.
5. **Adapting to Change:** Authentic leaders embrace change and guide their teams through transitions with clarity and purpose. By managing change effectively, they ensure the organization remains resilient in the face of market or environmental shifts.

The Role of Authentic Leadership in Fortune 500, Fortune 1000, and Government Organizations

- **Fortune 500:** Authentic leadership is particularly critical for large corporations where transparency and ethical leadership are essential for maintaining stakeholder trust. Authentic leaders in Fortune 500 companies help create a culture that attracts and retains top talent, encourages innovation, and builds lasting relationships with customers, investors, and other stakeholders. They also play a pivotal role in ensuring corporate social responsibility and sustainability practices are a priority.
- **Fortune 1000**: These organizations often face the challenge of competing with larger, more resource-rich companies. Authentic leadership helps establish a differentiated organizational culture that emphasizes integrity, employee development, and agility. Authentic leaders in these companies help their teams stay motivated and aligned with company goals, contributing to improved performance and growth.
- **Government Organizations:** In the public sector, authentic leadership can significantly improve accountability, citizen trust, and effective governance. Authentic leaders within government organizations are transparent in their decision-making, foster collaboration, and ensure that policies are developed and implemented ethically. This leads to more effective public service and builds greater community support.

How the DOGE (2025) Government Program Supports Change Management

The DOGE (2025) government program likely refers to an initiative aimed at fostering digital transformation and innovative solutions in the public sector. While the specific details of the program are not widely known, here's how a program like DOGE (2025) could support change management:

1. **Enabling Digital Transformation:** Programs like DOGE (2025) typically focus on modernizing government processes through technology. By implementing digital tools and platforms, the program can streamline operations, improve efficiency, and make change more manageable across large public sector organizations.
2. **Supporting Workforce Adaptation:** As governments introduce new technologies or processes, there is a need for continuous learning and skill development. Change management initiatives supported by programs like DOGE (2025) help employees adapt to new systems, encouraging a culture of innovation and growth.
3. **Fostering Collaboration and Communication:** Change management often fails when there's a lack of communication. A program like DOGE (2025) could focus on enhancing collaboration across different government departments and stakeholders, ensuring that all levels of government are aligned in implementing changes.
4. **Managing Stakeholder Expectations:** Government programs can also assist in managing public expectations during times of change. By clearly communicating the goals and benefits of the transformation, DOGE (2025) can help mitigate resistance to change and garner public support.

In summary, the DOGE (2025) (Department of Government Efficiency) program can support change management by offering structured initiatives that address digital transformation, workforce development, and cross-departmental collaboration, ensuring that change is effectively managed and successfully implemented.

The Government's Plan Regarding Organizational Change:

When a government introduces a Department of Government Efficiency (DOGE) or any program focused on organizational change, the primary objective is typically to modernize public sector operations, improve public services, and streamline bureaucratic processes to create more efficient, responsive, and citizen-focused organizations. Key aspects of such government initiatives include:

1. **Digitization and Technology Integration:** Governments often seek to digitize their operations, utilizing cloud computing, data analytics, and AI to automate and streamline processes. This helps reduce manual work, eliminate inefficiencies, and enhance citizen access to government services.
2. **Performance Management**: Implementing performance management systems allows governments to track outcomes and measure the efficiency of various departments. This often includes setting clear goals, monitoring progress, and using data to inform decision-making.
3. **Cost Reduction and Resource Optimization:** Government agencies often operate under budget constraints, so efficiency programs aim to reduce waste, streamline resource allocation, and optimize the use of taxpayer money. This could involve consolidating departments, reengineering processes, or eliminating redundant activities.
4. **Employee Empowerment and Development:** Organizational change often requires upskilling public employees and enhancing leadership. Governments typically invest in leadership development, training programs, and fostering a culture of innovation to equip employees to manage the changes successfully.
5. **Citizen-Centric Services:** Governments may seek to improve citizen engagement by creating more accessible and user-friendly systems. This could include introducing self-service platforms, digital government portals, and more responsive communication strategies to meet the needs of citizens.
6. **Change Management Frameworks:** Governments usually apply structured change management models to guide large-scale reforms. This may include frameworks such as Kotter's 8-Step Model, Lewin's Change Model, or others that emphasize communication, stakeholder buy-in, and gradual implementation.

How Sustainability Supports the Bundy Model for Organizations and Leaders

The Bundy Model (Control, Alt, and Delete) is an effective framework for facilitating organizational change and ensuring sustainability, particularly in government or large organizations. Let's apply it to creating a sustainable change environment in the context of government and organizational leadership:

1. **Control**
   - **Government Efficiency:** In the context of the Department of Government Efficiency (DOGE), Control means setting clear goals and expectations around the desired efficiencies and changes. Leaders should focus on controlling the implementation of best practices, technology, and performance standards to ensure the right processes are in place for success. It also means controlling resources such as budgets, technology, and personnel effectively.
   - **Sustainability Impact:** By controlling processes and resources, the organization can avoid waste, manage costs effectively, and ensure that the change initiatives are on track to meet long-term sustainability goals. Authentic leadership is key here—authentic leaders can ensure the team is motivated, aligned, and working toward the same objectives.
2. **Alt (Alternative Actions or Perspectives)**
   - **Government Efficiency:** The Alt step encourages organizations to explore alternative strategies for achieving efficiency. For example, governments may explore alternative solutions like digital tools or partnerships with private sectors for public services. It also involves being open to alternative perspectives and encouraging feedback from employees, citizens, and other stakeholders. This could include fostering innovation by allowing departments to propose and pilot new approaches.
   - **Sustainability Impact:** This step helps the organization be adaptive and resilient by continuously exploring new ways to improve operations. Leaders can help build an organizational culture of flexibility and innovation, ensuring that sustainability doesn't become stagnant but remains dynamic and forward-thinking. For example, by considering new technologies, governments can find more efficient ways to reduce costs or improve services in the long run.
3. **Delete**
   - **Government Efficiency:** Delete focuses on removing outdated processes, ineffective programs, or inefficiencies that no longer align with organizational goals. It could involve eliminating redundant programs, discontinuing manual or bureaucratic practices, and removing any obstacles that slow down the pace of change.
   - Sustainability Impact: By deleting what no longer serves the organization, governments can streamline operations and reduce unnecessary costs, freeing up resources for more sustainable initiatives. It also means deleting outdated leadership practices that no longer support organizational goals and replacing them with more authentic leadership practices that focus on transparency, communication, and employee engagement.
   they serve.

Supporting Sustainability with Authentic Leadership

Authentic leadership is key to ensuring sustainability in government and organizational change. Authentic leaders create environments where individuals feel empowered, valued, and part of a cohesive team. This leads to better employee retention, greater collaboration, and higher morale—all of which contribute to a sustainable organizational culture.
By using the Bundy Model in combination with authentic leadership, government organizations and leaders can:

- Foster trust through transparent decision-making.
- Engage employees by empowering them to contribute to change initiatives.
- Align organizational goals with individual values, creating a more sustainable and cohesive workforce.
- Adapt to changing circumstances by exploring alternative solutions and learning from failures.

Sustainability in government or large organizations can be achieved through strategic, methodical changes like those outlined in the Bundy Model. By focusing on authentic leadership and ensuring that employees are actively engaged in these changes, governments can create a sustainable future that benefits both employees and the public they serve.

The Role of Authentic Leadership in Long-Term Sustainability

The role of an authentic leader in achieving long-term success, particularly in relation to sustainability, is critical in shaping an organization's culture, strategy, and practices. Authentic leadership, with its focus on transparency, integrity, and ethical behavior, is an essential driver of sustainable success. Below, I'll explore how authentic leadership contributes to long-term success through the lens of sustainability, both in terms of environmental, social, and economic sustainability.

1. Building Trust and Organizational Resilience

One of the primary aspects of authentic leadership is the ability to foster trust among employees, stakeholders, and customers. This trust is built on transparency, open communication, and consistency between words and actions. For sustainability efforts to be effective, employees need to feel that their leaders are committed to long-term goals rather than short-term gains. This commitment to authenticity strengthens organizational resilience, enabling companies to endure external challenges like economic downturns, environmental crises, and shifts in market demands.

Impact on sustainability:

- Authentic leaders create a strong organizational culture based on trust, which ensures that sustainability practices are embraced across all levels of the organization.
- They provide a stable foundation during times of crisis, helping the organization to adapt, pivot, and recover.

2. Ethical Decision-Making and Long-Term Vision

Authentic leaders prioritize ethical decision-making, which is essential for sustainability. Their focus on values-based leadership encourages a long-term vision rather than immediate profits or outcomes. In the context of sustainability, this means leaders take into account the environmental, social, and economic consequences of their decisions. Authentic leaders also engage employees and stakeholders in the decision-making process, ensuring that everyone is aligned with the organization's sustainable goals.

Impact on sustainability:

- Ethical decision-making helps avoid practices that could harm the environment or exploit people, ensuring that the organization remains committed to sustainable development.
- By embedding sustainability into the core values of the organization, authentic leaders drive long-term strategies that ensure success and growth without compromising future generations' ability to thrive.

3. Inspiring Innovation and Employee Engagement

Authentic leadership encourages employee engagement by empowering individuals to contribute meaningfully to the organization's goals. Authentic leaders foster an environment where employees feel valued and motivated to innovate. In the context of sustainability, engaged employees are more likely to propose innovative solutions to reduce waste, improve energy efficiency, and create environmentally-friendly products or services.

Impact on sustainability:

- Engaged and empowered employees often come up with creative ideas and solutions for making the business more sustainable, reducing its ecological footprint, and promoting social responsibility.
- Leaders who are authentic in their commitment to sustainability inspire employees to adopt similar values, promoting a culture of innovation and continuous improvement in sustainable practices.

4. Long-Term Stakeholder Relationship:

Authentic leaders excel in building strong, trust-based relationships not just within the organization, but also with external stakeholders such as customers, suppliers, and the local community. These relationships are particularly important for sustainability, as they help organizations build credibility and ensure that their actions are aligned with societal expectations. A commitment to sustainability can build goodwill and strengthen the organization's reputation in the marketplace.

Impact on sustainability:

- Long-term stakeholder relationships are foundational to corporate social responsibility (CSR) initiatives, which are often integral to sustainability.
- Authentic leaders ensure that the company is seen as a responsible corporate citizen, which can lead to long-term profitability through customer loyalty, employee satisfaction, and positive brand reputation.

5. Leading by Example and Cultural Transformation

Authentic leaders lead by example. Their actions, behaviors, and decisions reflect their personal values, which often align with broader social and environmental responsibility goals. This is crucial in driving cultural transformation toward sustainability within the organization. Employees are more likely to adopt sustainable practices when they see their leaders modeling those behaviors. Authentic leaders don't just talk about sustainability; they actively live and promote it.

Impact on sustainability:

- By integrating sustainability into the leadership style, authentic leaders set the standard for behavior within the organization, creating a culture where sustainability is ingrained in daily operations and business strategies.
- Their consistent focus on sustainable actions sends a clear message to employees, customers, and investors that sustainability is a top priority.

or the planet.

6. Strategic Alignment and Accountability

Authentic leaders ensure that the sustainability goals of the organization are not just lofty ideals but are embedded into the business strategy. This includes setting measurable goals for reducing carbon footprints, improving supply chain ethics, or increasing diversity and inclusion. They are committed to accountability, ensuring that sustainability efforts are continuously tracked, evaluated, and adjusted to meet long-term goals.

Impact on sustainability:

- Authentic leaders integrate sustainability into the strategic planning process, making it an essential part of the organization's mission and vision.
- Their commitment to accountability ensures that sustainability objectives are achieved and that the organization's progress is transparent to stakeholders, helping to build trust and credibility.

7. Advocacy for Social and Environmental Impact

In addition to leading within the organization, authentic leaders often act as advocates for broader social and environmental change. They use their platforms and influence to encourage industry-wide shifts toward sustainability, support policies that protect the environment, and engage with communities to create positive change.

Impact on sustainability:

- Leaders who advocate for social and environmental causes create ripples beyond their organizations, influencing the entire industry or sector to adopt more sustainable practices.
- They can engage in collaborative efforts with other organizations, governments, and NGOs to drive collective action toward shared sustainability goals, ultimately contributing to a more sustainable society.

The Role of Authentic Leadership in Long-Term Sustainability

Authentic leadership plays a crucial role in promoting long-term sustainability by creating a culture of trust, ethical behavior, employee engagement, and accountability. By leading with integrity and aligning organizational goals with sustainability principles, authentic leaders ensure that their organizations are well-positioned for long-term success. They inspire innovation, build strong relationships, and advocate for broader societal change, all of which are essential for achieving sustainability in today's interconnected world.

In summary, authentic leadership is the cornerstone for embedding sustainability into an organization's DNA. Authentic leaders drive change by setting an example, engaging employees, and making ethical decisions that benefit both the organization and society as a whole, ensuring that long-term success is achieved without sacrificing the future of people

SUCCESSION AND LEADERSHIP

- THE JOURNEY TO SELF-DISCOVERY IN BUSINESS, IDENTIFYING CRITICAL ROLES AND POSITIONS
- CRITICAL ROLES AND POSITIONS IN THE JOURNEY TO SELF-DISCOVERY IN BUSINESS
- THE IMPORTANCE OF SELF-DISCOVERY IN BUSINESS LEADERSHIP
- SKILL DEVELOPMENT PROGRAMS
- MENTORSHIP AND COACHING (CONTROL, ALT, DELETE, AND RESET)
- CANDIDATE READINESS

CH.4

The Journey to Self-Discovery in Business, Identifying Critical Roles and Positions

Most Prominent Leadership Roles Actively Sought After in America and Their Salaries

In today's competitive job market, various leadership roles are in high demand across industries. Companies and organizations are seeking dynamic, visionary leaders who can drive innovation, manage teams, and align business objectives with long-term goals. Below are some of the most prominent leadership roles in America along with their average salaries:

Chief Executive Officer (CEO)

- **Role:** The CEO is the highest-ranking executive in an organization, responsible for overall strategy, decision-making, and operational management. They lead the company's direction, communicate with stakeholders, and ensure long-term profitability and sustainability.
- **Average Salary:** $180,000 to $250,000 per year, with the potential for bonuses and stock options (in larger companies, compensation can rise significantly, often into the millions).

Chief Financial Officer (CFO)

- **Role:** The CFO oversees the financial operations of an organization, including financial planning, risk management, record-keeping, and financial reporting. The CFO plays a critical role in strategic decision-making and securing the financial health of the business.
- **Average Salary:** $150,000 to $300,000 per year, depending on company size and industry.

Chief Operating Officer (COO)

- **Role:** The COO manages the day-to-day operations of an organization, ensuring that business functions run smoothly and efficiently. The COO often works closely with the CEO to implement strategic goals and improve operational processes.
- **Average Salary:** $150,000 to $250,000 per year.

Chief Marketing Officer (CMO)

- **Role:** The CMO leads the marketing department, developing and executing marketing strategies, brand management, and customer engagement initiatives. They are responsible for driving the company's brand identity and market positioning.
- **Average Salary:** $120,000 to $250,000 per year.

Chief Technology Officer (CTO)

- **Role:** The CTO leads technology and innovation within a company, overseeing IT infrastructure, software development, and technological strategy. This role has become more critical as companies increasingly depend on digital solutions and emerging technologies.
- **Average Salary:** $150,000 to $300,000 per year.

- **Human Resources Director/Chief Human Resources Officer (CHRO)**
  - **Role:** The CHRO oversees human resources strategies, talent acquisition, employee development, and company culture. They ensure that the organization has the right people in the right roles and supports a healthy work environment.
  - **Average Salary:** $120,000 to $250,000 per year.

General Manager (GM)
  - **Role:** The GM is responsible for overseeing operations and business performance within a specific department, division, or location. The GM ensures that goals and objectives are met and typically reports directly to the CEO or other executives.
  - **Average Salary:** $100,000 to $200,000 per year.

Product Manager/Director
  - **Role:** A product manager leads product development from concept to launch. This role requires a deep understanding of market trends, customer needs, and how to translate that into successful products.
  - **Average Salary:** $110,000 to $160,000 per year.

The Journey to Self-Discovery in Business: Identifying Critical Roles and Positions

The Journey to Self-Discovery in Business refers to the process in which individuals and organizations evaluate and understand their true purpose, strengths, values, and goals. It's about exploring the self, recognizing personal and professional aspirations, and aligning those with broader organizational objectives. This journey is crucial for personal growth, leadership development, and for driving the success of a business.

Critical Roles and Positions in the Journey to Self-Discovery in Business

Self-Reflective Leadership

Leaders on a self-discovery journey typically engage in deep introspection and emotional intelligence development. They understand their own motivations, values, and strengths, which can influence the culture and success of an organization. These leaders inspire self-awareness and encourage the same in their teams.

- **Critical Position:** CEO, COO, and CHRO. These roles require leaders to define the vision of the company and help others align their personal goals with organizational missions.

Visionary and Strategic Thinkers

A key part of self-discovery in business involves understanding how individual and organizational goals align. Leaders who can think strategically and envision the future of the company are crucial. This is particularly important in navigating changes, creating growth plans, and ensuring sustainability.

- **Critical Position:** CEO, CTO, and CMO. These individuals must not only know the direction the company needs to go but also understand how the changing business landscape can create new opportunities for growth.

Empathetic and Inspirational Leadership
Empathy plays a key role in the journey to self-discovery. Leaders must connect with employees, understand their personal challenges, and create a work environment that fosters trust and collaboration. Such leaders empower teams to share their aspirations and align those with business goals.

- **Critical Position:** CHRO, COO, and General Manager. These positions need to understand the human side of business, making decisions that reflect the well-being of employees while ensuring productivity.

Change Agents
In the journey to self-discovery, business leaders must also be adaptable and resilient. Change agents are individuals who champion change, whether it's adapting to new technology, shifting organizational culture, or restructuring business models.

- **Critical Position:** Product Manager, Chief Innovation Officer, or even a dedicated Chief Transformation Officer. These roles are integral to guiding businesses through change and maintaining organizational sustainability.

Mentors and Coaches
In the process of self-discovery, leaders also serve as mentors who guide others on their career paths. This involves understanding an individual's strengths and areas for development and providing the necessary guidance, training, and feedback to help them grow.

- **Critical Position:** HR Director, Leadership Development Manager, and Senior Executives. These roles focus on nurturing talent, developing leadership pipelines, and aligning personal growth with business objectives.

The Importance of Self-Discovery in Business Leadership

Self-discovery allows leaders to:

- **Align** personal values with the mission and vision of the company.
- **Develop** stronger relationships with employees, creating a collaborative and transparent culture.
- **Drive** innovation and forward-thinking strategies that lead to growth.
- **Build** organizational resilience by fostering adaptability and continuous learning.

The journey to self-discovery in business is not only about individual growth but also about shaping organizations that are purpose-driven and sustainable. Leaders who embark on this journey align their personal strengths and values with their roles, creating environments where employees feel empowered and motivated to contribute to long-term success. The critical roles identified—such as CEOs, CHROs, and Product Managers—serve as key players in this transformational journey, ensuring that organizations evolve in a way that balances both human and business needs.

Worksheet: Journey to Self-Discovery in Business & Defining Success Metrics for Leadership

Section 1: Self-Discovery Reflection for Business Leaders

Purpose: This section is designed to guide leaders in reflecting on their journey of self-discovery, personal strengths, and alignment with their business goals. This reflection will help them better understand their role in the organization and how they can lead with authenticity.

Instructions: Take time to reflect on the following questions and write your thoughts below.

1. **What are my core values?**

- **(Examples: Integrity, Transparency, Innovation, Collaboration)**
    -
    -
    -

2. **What motivates me as a leader?**

- **(Examples: Empowering others, Driving change, Achieving long-term success)**
    -
    -
    -

3. **What are my key strengths as a leader?**

- **(Examples: Strategic thinking, Emotional intelligence, Decision-making)**
    -
    -
    -

4. **What leadership traits do I admire in others, and how do I emulate them?**
    -
    -
    -

5. **What does success look like to me personally and professionally?**
    -
    -
    -

Section 2: Key Leadership Roles and Critical Success Factors

Purpose: This section helps you assess the key leadership roles in your organization and define the success metrics for each role.

Instructions: For each of the leadership positions listed below, outline the key responsibilities and define what success looks like for you in that role.

1. **Chief Executive Officer (CEO)**

- **Key Responsibilities:**
    -

- **Success Metrics:(Examples: Company growth, profitability, employee satisfaction, market share)**
    -
    -

2. **Chief Financial Officer (CFO)**
- **Key Responsibilities:**
    -
- **Success Metrics:(Examples: Financial performance, cost savings, budget accuracy)**
    -
    -

3. **Chief Operating Officer (COO)**
- **Key Responsibilities:**
    -
- **Success Metrics:(Examples: Operational efficiency, process improvement, employee performance)**
    -
    -

4. **Chief Marketing Officer (CMO)**
- **Key Responsibilities:**
    -
- **Success Metrics:(Examples: Brand awareness, customer acquisition, ROI on marketing campaigns)**
    -
    -

5. **Chief Technology Officer (CTO)**
- **Key Responsibilities:**
    -
- **Success Metrics:(Examples: Technology innovation, system uptime, software development timelines)**
    -
    -

Section 3: Defining Success Metrics for Leadership in Sustainability
Purpose: This section focuses on defining success metrics for leadership positions specifically tied to sustainability efforts within the organization. Sustainability here is viewed through environmental, social, and economic lenses.
Instructions: For each role, identify sustainability-related goals and how you will measure their success.

CEO: Sustainability Vision and Strategy

- Sustainability Goals:(Examples: Reducing carbon footprint, achieving diversity and inclusion targets, community engagement)
    -

Success Metrics:(Examples: Carbon footprint reduction percentage, diversity percentage increase, community initiatives impact)

-
-

CFO: Financial and Environmental Sustainability

Sustainability Goals:(Examples: Investment in sustainable projects, financial impact of green technologies)

-
-

Success Metrics:(Examples: ROI on sustainable investments, reduction in resource costs, budget allocation to green initiatives)

-
-

COO: Operational Efficiency and Resource Management

Sustainability Goals:(Examples: Reducing waste, improving supply chain sustainability, increasing energy efficiency)

-
-

Success Metrics:(Examples: Waste reduction percentage, energy savings, supplier sustainability audits)

-
-

CMO: Brand Sustainability and Consumer Engagement

Sustainability Goals:(Examples: Promoting eco-friendly products, engaging customers in sustainability efforts)

-
-

Success Metrics:(Examples: Customer satisfaction with sustainability efforts, increase in sustainable product sales, positive brand perception)

-
-

Section 4: Action Plan for Aligning Leadership Success with Organizational Sustainability

- **Purpose:** This section guides leaders to take actionable steps toward aligning their leadership approach with the long-term sustainability goals of the organization.
- **Instructions:** Create an action plan based on your self-discovery, the leadership positions in your organization, and the sustainability goals. Set a timeline for achieving these actions.

What actions will I take to align my leadership style with organizational sustainability?

-
-
-

How can I inspire and empower my team to embrace sustainability?

-
-
-

What steps will I take to ensure continuous feedback and adaptation in sustainability efforts?

-
-
-

Timeline for Implementation:
(Example: Quarterly reviews, annual sustainability reports, monthly team meetings)

-
-

Final Reflection and Commitment
Purpose: Reflect on your journey to self-discovery and leadership development. Reaffirm your commitment to your personal growth and to achieving the sustainability goals within your organization.

1. How has this process of self-discovery shaped my leadership approach?

-
-

2. What will I do differently moving forward to ensure I lead with authenticity and sustainability in mind?

-
-

This worksheet can be a valuable tool for business leaders seeking to align their personal growth with organizational success, particularly in areas of sustainability and effective leadership. It encourages reflection, goal setting, and a structured approach to leadership development.

Skill Development Programs

Skill Development Programs for Authentic Leaders in Today's Economic Society

In today's rapidly changing economic landscape, authentic leadership has become an essential quality for driving long-term organizational success. Authentic leaders are those who lead with transparency, integrity, self-awareness, and ethical practices. Developing the skills necessary for authentic leadership not only improves individual leadership capacity but also fosters a thriving organizational culture. Below are key skill development programs that can help cultivate authentic leadership in today's economic society:

1. Emotional Intelligence (EI) Training

Why It's Important: Emotional intelligence is a cornerstone of authentic leadership. Authentic leaders must be able to understand and manage their own emotions, as well as empathize with and manage the emotions of others. In today's economic society, where the work environment can be stressful and volatile, emotional intelligence allows leaders to remain calm under pressure and build strong interpersonal relationships.

Skills Covered:

- Self-awareness and self-regulation
- Empathy and understanding others' emotions
- Effective communication
- Conflict resolution and stress management

Program Example:

- Daniel Goleman's Emotional Intelligence Training Program: Based on the work of Daniel Goleman, this program helps leaders enhance their emotional intelligence by learning to manage emotions effectively, build emotional rapport, and communicate with empathy.

2. Ethical Leadership Development

Why It's Important: In an era of corporate scandals and public scrutiny, authentic leaders are expected to model ethical behavior and create a culture of integrity. Ethical leadership development equips leaders with the tools to make decisions that are not only profitable but also responsible, fostering trust among stakeholders.

Skills Covered:

- Ethical decision-making frameworks
- Corporate social responsibility (CSR)
- Developing a values-based leadership style
- Leading with integrity and transparency

Program Example:

- Harvard Kennedy School's Executive Education on Ethical Leadership: This program focuses on equipping leaders with the knowledge and frameworks to lead with a strong ethical compass, guiding organizations through complex ethical dilemmas in a global economy.

3. Authentic Communication Skills

Why It's Important: Authentic leaders must communicate openly and honestly with their teams, fostering an environment of trust and transparency. Effective communication is particularly critical in today's digital and globalized economy, where leaders need to navigate diverse teams and various channels of communication.

Skills Covered:

- Authentic communication and storytelling
- Active listening and feedback techniques
- Communicating with clarity and purpose
- Handling difficult conversations and conflicts with transparency

Program Example:

- Dale Carnegie's Leadership Training for Managers: This program helps leaders enhance their communication and interpersonal skills, with a focus on building trust, enhancing listening abilities, and communicating authentically with various stakeholders.

4. Leadership and Organizational Change Management

Why It's Important: Economic shifts and digital transformation require leaders to adapt quickly and effectively. Authentic leaders need to manage change in a way that is not only efficient but also transparent and empathetic, ensuring that employees remain engaged and motivated throughout transitions.

Skills Covered:

- Change management strategies and frameworks
- Leading through uncertainty and ambiguity
- Creating a resilient organizational culture
- Supporting employee well-being during transitions

Program Example:

- Prosci Change Management Certification Program: This certification equips leaders with the tools to manage organizational change successfully, focusing on the human side of change and how to lead with authenticity through transitions.

5. Strategic Thinking and Visionary Leadership
Why It's Important: In today's complex and competitive economy, authentic leaders must have a clear, long-term vision for their organizations. They must be able to balance short-term goals with long-term sustainability and navigate complex decision-making landscapes with a focus on purpose and societal impact.

Skills Covered:

- Visionary and strategic thinking
- Long-term goal setting and planning
- Problem-solving and decision-making
- Aligning personal values with organizational objectives

Program Example:

- INSEAD Executive Education on Strategy and Leadership: This program helps leaders develop a strategic mindset by focusing on the interplay between organizational goals and external market factors, fostering a vision-driven approach to leadership.

6. Diversity, Equity, and Inclusion (DEI) Training
Why It's Important: Authentic leaders must prioritize diversity, equity, and inclusion (DEI) in their organizations to foster a culture of respect, belonging, and fairness. In today's diverse and interconnected world, leaders need to develop inclusive leadership practices to create workplaces that celebrate diversity and promote equality.

Skills Covered:

- Understanding and addressing unconscious bias
- Creating an inclusive culture
- Leading diverse teams
- Implementing DEI initiatives and policies

Program Example:

- Cornell University's Diversity and Inclusion Certificate Program: This program teaches leaders how to lead with inclusivity, addressing the challenges of unconscious bias and building more diverse and equitable organizations.

7. Coaching and Mentoring for Leadership Development
Why It's Important: Authentic leaders often engage in coaching and mentoring to develop the leadership potential of others. These programs not only improve leadership effectiveness but also create a culture of continuous learning and personal development.

Skills Covered:

- Coaching techniques and frameworks
- Mentorship best practices
- Feedback and performance management
- Developing leadership potential in others environment.

Program Example:

- Harvard Kennedy School's Executive Education on Ethical Leadership: This program focuses on equipping leaders with the knowledge and frameworks to lead with a strong ethical compass, guiding organizations through complex ethical dilemmas in a global economy.

3. Authentic Communication Skills

Why It's Important: Authentic leaders must communicate openly and honestly with their teams, fostering an environment of trust and transparency. Effective communication is particularly critical in today's digital and globalized economy, where leaders need to navigate diverse teams and various channels of communication.

Skills Covered:

- Authentic communication and storytelling
- Active listening and feedback techniques
- Communicating with clarity and purpose
- Handling difficult conversations and conflicts with transparency

Program Example:

- Dale Carnegie's Leadership Training for Managers: This program helps leaders enhance their communication and interpersonal skills, with a focus on building trust, enhancing listening abilities, and communicating authentically with various stakeholders.

4. Leadership and Organizational Change Management

Why It's Important: Economic shifts and digital transformation require leaders to adapt quickly and effectively. Authentic leaders need to manage change in a way that is not only efficient but also transparent and empathetic, ensuring that employees remain engaged and motivated throughout transitions.

Skills Covered:

- Change management strategies and frameworks
- Leading through uncertainty and ambiguity
- Creating a resilient organizational culture
- Supporting employee well-being during transitions

Program Example:

- Prosci Change Management Certification Program: This certification equips leaders with the tools to manage organizational change successfully, focusing on the human side of change and how to lead with authenticity through transitions.

5. Strategic Thinking and Visionary Leadership
Why It's Important: In today's complex and competitive economy, authentic leaders must have a clear, long-term vision for their organizations. They must be able to balance short-term goals with long-term sustainability and navigate complex decision-making landscapes with a focus on purpose and societal impact.

Skills Covered:

- Visionary and strategic thinking
- Long-term goal setting and planning
- Problem-solving and decision-making
- Aligning personal values with organizational objectives

Program Example:

- INSEAD Executive Education on Strategy and Leadership: This program helps leaders develop a strategic mindset by focusing on the interplay between organizational goals and external market factors, fostering a vision-driven approach to leadership.

6. Diversity, Equity, and Inclusion (DEI) Training
Why It's Important: Authentic leaders must prioritize diversity, equity, and inclusion (DEI) in their organizations to foster a culture of respect, belonging, and fairness. In today's diverse and interconnected world, leaders need to develop inclusive leadership practices to create workplaces that celebrate diversity and promote equality.

Skills Covered:

- Understanding and addressing unconscious bias
- Creating an inclusive culture
- Leading diverse teams
- Implementing DEI initiatives and policies

Program Example:

- Cornell University's Diversity and Inclusion Certificate Program: This program teaches leaders how to lead with inclusivity, addressing the challenges of unconscious bias and building more diverse and equitable organizations.

7. Coaching and Mentoring for Leadership Development
Why It's Important: Authentic leaders often engage in coaching and mentoring to develop the leadership potential of others. These programs not only improve leadership effectiveness but also create a culture of continuous learning and personal development.

Skills Covered:

- Coaching techniques and frameworks
- Mentorship best practices
- Feedback and performance management
- Developing leadership potential in others environment.

Program Example:

- Center for Creative Leadership's Coaching for Leadership Development Program: This program focuses on improving coaching and mentoring skills, helping leaders guide their teams with authenticity, empathy, and purpose.

8. Resilience and Stress Management for Leaders

Why It's Important: The economic challenges of the 21st century—such as uncertainty, market volatility, and technological disruption—demand leaders who can remain resilient in the face of adversity. Authentic leaders must manage stress effectively and foster resilience within their teams to maintain productivity and morale.

Skills Covered:

- Stress management techniques
- Building personal resilience and team resilience
- Mindfulness practices for leaders
- Navigating failure and setbacks with authenticity

Program Example:

- Mindful Leadership Training by Search Inside Yourself: This program uses mindfulness-based techniques to help leaders manage stress, develop resilience, and lead with clarity and authenticity under pressure.

9. Innovation and Creativity Leadership

Why It's Important: To lead effectively in today's economy, authentic leaders need to cultivate a culture of innovation. Leaders must inspire creativity and foster an environment where new ideas can flourish, ensuring the organization adapts to changing market needs.

Skills Covered:

- Encouraging creativity and innovation
- Leading teams in brainstorming and problem-solving
- Turning innovative ideas into actionable strategies
- Managing risk in the innovation process

Program Example:

- MIT Sloan School of Management's Leading Innovation Program: This program equips leaders with the tools to foster a culture of innovation, inspiring teams to think creatively and strategically in today's fast-paced economic environment.

Mentorship and Coaching According to the Bundy Model (Control, Alt, Delete, and Reset)

The Bundy Model (Control, Alt, Delete, and Reset) is a metaphor for how individuals and organizations can approach continuous development, transformation, and overcoming challenges. It aligns well with the concept of mentorship and coaching in leadership development, as it encourages individuals to make intentional changes, self-reflect, and reset their approach to ensure ongoing growth. Here's how the Bundy Model can be applied to mentorship and coaching in the context of skill development:

1. Control: Establishing Leadership Competencies and Areas for Growth

In the Bundy Model, "Control" refers to identifying where you currently stand and what you want to control or change. In the context of mentorship and coaching, this phase focuses on understanding one's current skill set, identifying areas of strength, and pinpointing areas for development. A key part of this is leveraging mentorship to help you gain perspective on your leadership style, skills, and performance.

- **Mentorship's Role:**
    - A mentor in this phase can guide you through self-assessment, identifying your leadership competencies, and helping you understand where your strengths and weaknesses lie. The mentor can provide feedback from their experience, allowing you to control your professional development effectively.
    - Coaching in this phase is more action-oriented. A coach helps you assess your current performance and competencies and defines the specific skills you want to enhance. This can include refining communication, decision-making, emotional intelligence, or other core leadership traits.

- **Skill Development Application:**
    - Mentorship helps you gain clarity about your role and how your current competencies align with your leadership goals.
    - Coaching then provides tools, techniques, and frameworks to control and fine-tune those competencies to better fit your desired future trajectory.

2. Alt: Adapting to New Skills and Approaches

"Alt" in the Bundy Model stands for altering your course when necessary—making adjustments to your mindset or behaviors based on new knowledge and insights. Here, mentorship and coaching come into play by helping individuals adapt to new strategies, methods, or skills to meet evolving demands.

- **Mentorship's Role:**
  - A mentor provides insight into how to adapt to new challenges and change, drawing from their wealth of experience. They may guide you on how to pivot or adapt your leadership style when facing challenges like technological disruptions, organizational shifts, or changing market conditions.
  - Mentors often offer broader perspectives, helping you see patterns that you may not have noticed before.

- **Coaching's Role:**
  - Coaching in this phase is about accelerating adaptability. It focuses on helping you develop flexibility and resilience when adapting to new environments, roles, or challenges. Coaches may use situational exercises and real-time feedback to assist you in adjusting your approach to leadership.
  - Coaching often includes tools for managing stress, communication, or decision-making under change, giving you the ability to adapt effectively and confidently.

- **Skill Development Application:**
  - Mentorship aids in fostering an adaptive mindset, encouraging you to see change as an opportunity rather than a setback.
  - Coaching pushes for practical implementation, offering real-time feedback and constructive criticism that helps you adapt and refine new skills as you apply them.

3. Delete: Letting Go of Limiting Beliefs and Past Habits

"Delete" in the Bundy Model represents eliminating outdated behaviors, mindsets, or practices that no longer serve you or your organization. In terms of mentorship and coaching, this phase involves letting go of negative habits or limiting beliefs that can hinder your development.

- **Mentorship's Role:**
  - A mentor helps you identify unproductive patterns in your leadership style—such as poor communication habits, resistance to change, or fear of failure—that could be limiting your growth. They offer advice on how to break free from these behaviors.
  - The mentor may also share their own experiences of overcoming limiting beliefs, offering you strategies and wisdom for growth.
- **Coaching's Role:**
  - A coach works with you to break through mental barriers, focusing on changing behaviors that limit performance. Through specialized coaching techniques, such as cognitive reframing or performance-based feedback, the coach helps you overcome self-doubt, perfectionism, or other obstacles that may hold you back.
- **Skill Development Application:**
  - Mentorship allows you to see the areas where you may have been repeating ineffective habits, so you can consciously make the decision to change.
  - Coaching then helps you take deliberate actions to reframe and remove these limiting behaviors and mindset, helping you reach your full leadership potential.

4. Reset: Reimagining Leadership and Moving Forward with Renewed Purpose
"Reset" is about starting fresh, recalibrating, and making new commitments with greater clarity and focus. After identifying areas to control, adapting, and eliminating barriers, leaders reset to take purposeful action toward their next set of goals. In this phase, mentorship and coaching provide guidance, support, and accountability to move forward.

- **Mentorship's Role:**
    - A mentor helps you reset your leadership vision, offering perspective on how to align your current goals with your broader career trajectory. They can help you refine your long-term vision and set realistic milestones to achieve your goals.
    - Mentors also provide valuable advice on how to maintain a sense of purpose and stay committed to your leadership path.

- **Coaching's Role:**
    - Coaching is forward-focused, helping you set specific, actionable goals that support your reset strategy. This may include skill development plans, leadership action steps, or goal-setting frameworks.
    - A coach can also help you track progress, adjust goals as needed, and keep you accountable, ensuring you remain on track toward sustained growth.

- **Skill Development Application:**
    - Mentorship gives you strategic insights on where to focus your energy for maximum growth, ensuring your reset is aligned with both organizational needs and personal aspirations.
    - Coaching helps ensure that the reset is actionable, supporting you with tactics to implement your new plan and sustain growth long-term.

Where to Find Mentorship and Coaching

- **Mentorship:**
    - **Within Your Organization:** Look for senior leaders or colleagues with experience in areas where you need guidance. Many organizations have formal mentorship programs, so inquire about available opportunities.

    - **Professional Networks and Associations**: Join industry-specific groups or associations where you can connect with mentors who have expertise in your field.

    - **Online Platforms**: Websites like LinkedIn, Meetup, and MentorCruise connect individuals with mentors across various industries.

- **Coaching:**
  - **Executive Coaching Firms:** Many organizations hire professional coaches through coaching firms like BetterUp, Marshall Goldsmith Group, or The Center for Creative Leadership.
  - **Personal Development Coaches:** Coaches are available online or through platforms like Coach.me, Tony Robbins Coaching, or International Coach Federation (ICF) accredited coaches.
  - **Company-Provided Coaching:** Some companies offer internal coaching programs for leadership development, where coaches help guide you through organizational change and personal development.

Frequency of Mentorship and Coaching

To maintain and enhance one's credentials, mentorship and coaching should be ongoing, with frequency depending on your leadership goals and development stage.

- **Mentorship Frequency:**
  - Quarterly or Biannually: Mentorship should be structured to provide periodic check-ins, helping you navigate key milestones or challenges. This ensures continuous growth, guidance, and the reinforcement of your leadership journey.

- **Coaching Frequency:**
  - Monthly or Biweekly: Coaching sessions are more regular and focused on real-time skills development. Monthly or biweekly sessions provide actionable steps, feedback, and progress assessments to maintain forward momentum.
  - Ad-hoc sessions: Whenever you face a major transition, challenge, or need to reset your strategy, coaching can be particularly valuable for focused, intensive support.

Incorporating mentorship and coaching through the Bundy Model (Control, Alt, Delete, Reset) enables leaders to continuously evolve by gaining insights, adapting to change, eliminating limiting behaviors, and resetting their leadership approach. Mentorship offers long-term guidance, while coaching provides actionable steps for personal and professional growth. Regular engagement in these processes, combined with consistent self-reflection, will ensure that leaders stay relevant and prepared to meet the demands of today's dynamic business landscape.

Candidate Readiness

Candidate Readiness According to the Bundy Model (Control, Alt, Delete, and Reset)
The Bundy Model (Control, Alt, Delete, and Reset) provides a framework for self-reflection, adaptation, and growth. Applying this model to Candidate Readiness can help identify how candidates are prepared for roles, especially leadership positions, and how they can develop essential skills throughout their careers. The Bundy Model helps assess whether candidates are truly ready to take on roles, not just in terms of technical knowledge but also leadership qualities, mindset, and adaptability.

1. Control: Understanding Current Readiness and Skills

In the "Control" phase, individuals need to take stock of their current readiness. This means understanding where they are in their career and what competencies they have that qualify them for leadership or specialized roles. The process of self-assessment plays a key role here, as candidates must evaluate their existing skills, experience, and qualifications against the expectations of the roles they are pursuing.

Candidate Readiness in Control

Skill Development Focus: Candidates must assess their core skills, experience, and behaviors to determine where they stand in terms of readiness. Are they equipped with the necessary technical expertise? Are they prepared to manage teams or make high-level decisions?

Mentorship Role: Mentors can help candidates recognize their current skill gaps and advise on specific areas for improvement. A mentor may suggest areas where the candidate can develop further to be truly ready for a higher position.

Coaching Role: A coach works with the candidate to help them hone specific competencies, such as leadership, emotional intelligence, communication, or strategic thinking, ensuring they have the right tools and capabilities to excel in their role.

- **How to Apply for Skill Development:**

Perform a skills audit to identify strengths and weaknesses.
Develop a plan to enhance skills that are lacking, using targeted learning programs or on-the-job experience.
Use feedback from mentors and coaches to assess if the candidate is on track for their desired role.

2. Alt: Adapting and Evolving Skill Sets

- In the "Alt" phase, candidates are required to adapt to new challenges and demands. This phase involves modifying their approach, expanding their knowledge, and adapting to industry or role-specific changes. Adaptability is a critical skill, as candidates must be prepared for evolving responsibilities or entirely new roles that might demand flexibility, creativity, and innovation.

- **Candidate Readiness in Alt:**

Skill Development Focus: Candidates need to adjust their current capabilities to meet the demands of future roles. For example, a leader might need to shift from managing small teams to overseeing large divisions, requiring a whole new skill set in terms of management, strategy, and negotiation.

Mentorship Role: Mentors can provide advice on how to pivot and adapt skills for new or challenging situations. They can share personal stories of adapting to change and provide insight into how to maintain momentum in the face of new challenges.

Coaching Role: Coaches focus on developing adaptive strategies, and helping candidates prepare for upcoming challenges in their career path. This could involve stretch assignments or simulated environments where candidates practice adaptability and leadership under new circumstances.

- **How to Apply to Skill Development:**

Engage in cross-functional projects or rotational programs to broaden skills.

Take part in scenario-based coaching or simulation exercises that challenge current skillsets and promote new approaches.

Encourage continuous learning through industry-specific workshops or certifications to stay up-to-date with evolving skills in the industry.

3. Delete: Identifying and Letting Go of Limiting Behaviors or Skills

The "Delete" phase in the Bundy Model is about removing outdated skills, negative habits, or limiting beliefs that may hinder progress. For a candidate to be truly ready for the next level, they must be willing to eliminate counterproductive behaviors or outdated knowledge. This might include unproductive mindsets, lack of confidence, or failure to adopt new technologies that are critical to the role.

- **Candidate Readiness in Delete:**

Skill Development Focus: Candidates must confront behaviors or attitudes that are holding them back. They may need to delete outdated ways of thinking or approaches that no longer fit their future roles (e.g., outdated technical skills, lack of leadership acumen).

Mentorship Role: A mentor can help the candidate identify bad habits and point out areas that may be limiting their growth. The mentor may provide advice on how to shed negative patterns and adopt a mindset that is aligned with future goals.

Coaching Role: Coaches assist in helping candidates overcome mental barriers or negative beliefs (such as fear of failure or perfectionism). They work on behavioral modification, helping candidates replace ineffective behaviors with productive habits.

- **How to Apply to Skill Development:**

Perform a personal audit to identify any behaviors or skills that are outdated or hindering progress.

Use feedback from peers, supervisors, and coaches to uncover areas where improvement is needed.

Engage in training programs that address specific skill deficiencies or habits, such as public speaking, time management, or conflict resolution.

4. Reset: Reassessing Readiness and Recalibrating for the Future

In the "Reset" phase, candidates reassess their career goals, recalibrate their approach, and focus on new objectives. After working through the Control, Alt, and Delete stages, resetting allows candidates to refocus on their goals and ensure they are truly ready for the next step in their career.

- **Candidate Readiness in Reset:**

Skill Development Focus: Candidates need to reassess their readiness after undergoing various stages of development. Are they now prepared for the challenges of their new role? Have they acquired the necessary skills and mindset for success in this role?

Mentorship Role: Mentors can help candidates take a step back and evaluate their progress. They can offer advice on how to maintain momentum and keep a long-term perspective on leadership and career growth.

Coaching Role: Coaches help candidates establish a reset strategy for the future, focusing on new goals, vision, and specific next steps for leadership development. Coaches also support goal-setting and progress tracking to ensure continued success.

- **How to Apply to Skill Development:**

Engage in goal-setting exercises to recalibrate professional aspirations.

Work with mentors and coaches to develop a roadmap for ongoing development.

Set new performance benchmarks for yourself, and track progress over time to ensure readiness for new challenges.

- **Coaching Role:** Coaches assist in helping candidates overcome mental barriers or negative beliefs (such as fear of failure or perfectionism). They work on behavioral modification, helping candidates replace ineffective behaviors with productive habits.

- H**ow to Apply to Skill Development:**

Perform a personal audit to identify any behaviors or skills that are outdated or hindering progress.

Use feedback from peers, supervisors, and coaches to uncover areas where improvement is needed.

Engage in training programs that address specific skill deficiencies or habits, such as public speaking, time management, or conflict resolution.

- **4. Reset: Reassessing Readiness and Recalibrating for the Future**
- In the "Reset" phase, candidates reassess their career goals, recalibrate their approach, and focus on new objectives. After working through the Control, Alt, and Delete stages, resetting allows candidates to refocus on their goals and ensure they are truly ready for the next step in their career.

Candidate Readiness in Reset:

- **Skill Development Focus:** Candidates need to reassess their readiness after undergoing various stages of development. Are they now prepared for the challenges of their new role? Have they acquired the necessary skills and mindset for success in this role?
- **Mentorship Role:** Mentors can help candidates take a step back and evaluate their progress. They can offer advice on how to maintain momentum and keep a long-term perspective on leadership and career growth.

- **Coaching Role:** Coaches help candidates establish a reset strategy for the future, focusing on new goals, vision, and specific next steps for leadership development. Coaches also support goal-setting and progress tracking to ensure continued success.

- **How to Apply to Skill Development:**
- Engage in goal-setting exercises to recalibrate professional aspirations.
- Work with mentors and coaches to develop a roadmap for ongoing development.
- Set new performance benchmarks for yourself, and track progress over time to ensure readiness for new challenges.

Where to Find Candidate Readiness Support (Mentorship and Coaching)

Mentorship:

- **Within the Organization:** Senior leaders or colleagues who can offer insights and guidance on career growth and readiness for higher roles.
- **Professional Associations:** Many industries offer mentorship programs where experienced professionals help guide less experienced candidates toward greater success.
- **Online Platforms:** Platforms such as LinkedIn, MentorCruise, and Meetup offer opportunities to connect with mentors from various industries and sectors.
- Coaching:
- **Executive Coaching Firms:** Many organizations hire coaches through firms like BetterUp, The Center for Creative Leadership, or Marshall Goldsmith Group.
- **Independent Coaches:** Independent coaches specializing in leadership, skill development, and readiness can be found through platforms like Coach.me, ICF-certified coaches, or through personal referrals.
- **Internal Coaching Programs:** Some companies offer internal coaching to develop leadership talent and enhance candidate readiness for future roles.

Frequency of Mentorship and Coaching to Maintain Readiness

Mentorship Frequency:

- **Quarterly or Bi-Annually:** Mentorship sessions can be scheduled periodically to provide long-term guidance, assess progress, and adjust goals accordingly. This helps maintain readiness over time.
- **Ad-hoc:** Mentors should be consulted as needed when a major career transition, skill gap, or challenge arises.

Coaching Frequency:

- **Monthly or Biweekly:** Coaching sessions should be more frequent in nature, focusing on specific skill development and ensuring that readiness for the next level is maintained. Monthly or biweekly check-ins help address immediate challenges and ensure continual growth.
- **Intensive Coaching:** During critical transitions or leadership development stages, more frequent or intensive coaching (e.g., weekly sessions) may be required to ensure readiness.

Applying Candidate Readiness to the Bundy Model (Control, Alt, Delete, Reset) allows candidates to assess their current capabilities, adapt to new challenges, eliminate ineffective behaviors, and recalibrate their goals to ensure long-term success. Mentorship and coaching are critical tools that support each stage of readiness, guiding individuals toward effective personal and professional growth. By continually assessing and refining skills, candidates can ensure they are always prepared for the next phase of their career and leadership development.

Leadership Perspective and Looking Forward

The Bundy Model—comprising Control, Alt, Delete, and Reset—serves as a transformative framework for leadership development, strategic decision-making, and continuous personal and organizational growth. Developed by Dr. Kindall Bundy, this model emphasizes the need for leaders to regularly assess their positions, adapt to change, remove outdated or limiting behaviors, and reset their strategies to meet the dynamic needs of the business landscape. From Dr. Bundy's perspective, authentic leadership is a cornerstone for ensuring long-term organizational success. It underscores the importance of self-awareness, emotional intelligence, and ethical decision-making. Leaders who adopt an authentic approach build trust and foster a culture of transparency, empowerment, and resilience. They are committed to personal and professional development, understanding that their leadership impacts not only individual performance but the broader organization's culture, productivity, and sustainability.

1. Control: Foundation for Effective Leadership and Succession

In the Control phase of the Bundy Model, leaders assess their competencies and capabilities, identifying areas of strength and development. Dr. Bundy emphasizes the importance of this phase in leadership development, as it provides the foundation for long-term success. Leaders need to understand their current skill set and how it aligns with both their personal goals and organizational objectives. Authentic leadership emerges here, where leaders are deeply aware of their values and lead with integrity. By mentoring and coaching, leaders can ensure that their team members are similarly empowered to evaluate their own readiness for leadership roles. This phase is critical in succession planning, as identifying emerging leaders within the organization ensures that there is a pipeline of talent ready to step into key roles when needed.

2. Alt: Adaptation and Change Management

The Alt phase focuses on adaptability—the ability to pivot and evolve in response to new challenges and opportunities. In an ever-changing business environment, authentic leaders must be agile, demonstrating the ability to adjust their leadership style to address shifting market dynamics, technological advancements, and organizational restructuring. This phase encourages leaders to foster a culture of innovation and resilience, where learning and growth are ongoing processes. As part of succession planning, developing future-ready leaders who can swiftly adapt to new roles, technologies, and environments ensures the organization remains competitive and sustainable. Dr. Bundy's model highlights that adaptation is not merely about responding to change but leading it with foresight and clarity.

3. Delete: Eliminating Outdated Behaviors and Mindsets

The Delete phase is about recognizing and eliminating behaviors, practices, or mindsets that hinder personal and organizational progress. Dr. Bundy asserts that to succeed, leaders must periodically reflect on and remove limiting beliefs, ineffective strategies, and outdated practices that no longer serve the organization's objectives. In the context of leadership and succession, this phase is essential for addressing organizational inertia and fostering a culture of continuous improvement. Authentic leaders who embrace the "Delete" phase are unafraid to challenge their own assumptions and biases, ensuring they make data-driven, objective decisions. This mindset also supports the growth of emerging leaders, encouraging them to step into roles free of outdated practices and with a fresh perspective on how to lead.

4. Reset: Recalibration and Vision for the Future
In the Reset phase, Dr. Bundy highlights the importance of recalibrating leadership strategies to align with both current and future organizational needs. This phase involves setting new goals, refining approaches, and ensuring that the leadership vision remains relevant in a constantly evolving business environment. By resetting, leaders are able to adopt a forward-looking perspective, ensuring that both they and their organizations are prepared for future challenges. From a succession planning standpoint, the Reset phase ensures that future leaders are not only ready to take on current challenges but are also poised to lead through future uncertainty and evolving business landscapes.

Leadership Perspective on Succession and Forward-Looking Solutions

Dr. Bundy's Bundy Model positions authentic leadership as the catalyst for organizational success and sustainability. By continuously engaging in the four phases—Control, Alt, Delete, and Reset—leaders are empowered to navigate change, inspire innovation, and cultivate environments where future leaders thrive. The model provides a robust framework for developing a strong leadership pipeline, ensuring that organizations have the leadership talent needed for effective succession planning.

In today's business environment, where change management, talent retention, and organizational adaptability are critical to success, the Bundy Model provides a holistic approach that can drive long-term sustainability. By focusing on authentic leadership and fostering a culture of continuous learning and improvement, organizations can cultivate leaders who are not only prepared for current challenges but are forward-thinking and ready to lead into the future.

Ultimately, Dr. Bundy's work emphasizes that successful succession is not merely about filling positions but about preparing individuals to lead with authenticity, resilience, and a vision for sustainable growth. The Bundy Model, with its emphasis on leadership readiness, adaptability, and growth, equips organizations with the tools they need to ensure a future-ready leadership pipeline that will carry the organization toward success and sustainability.

RESOURCES FOR THE FUTURE LEADER

*BONUS

FD&Y CONSULTANTS

BURNOUT PREVENTION

A WORKBOOK FOR EMBRACING INTENTIONALITY AND OVERCOMING TOXIC PRODUCTIVITY

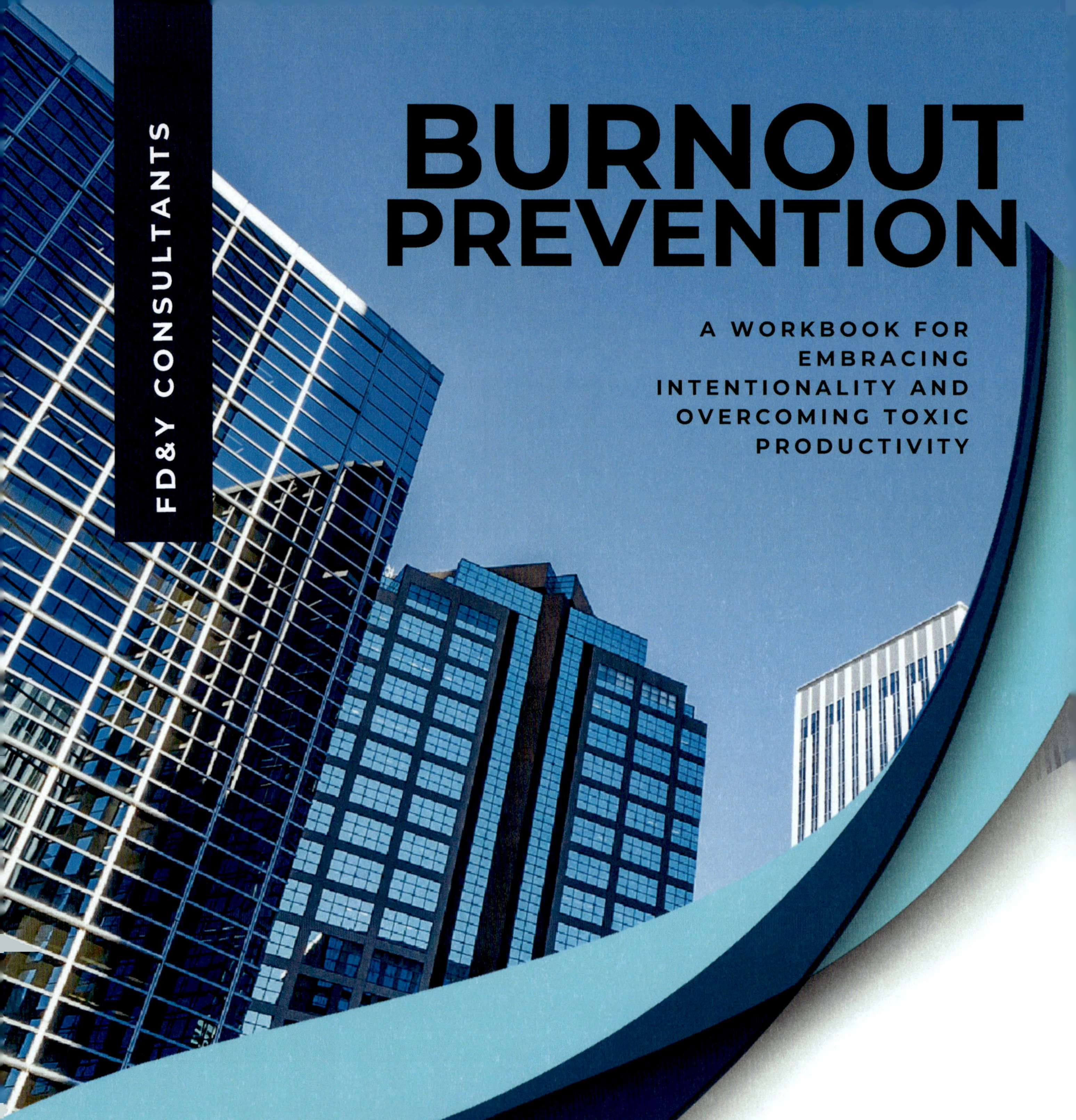

Table of
CONTENTS

Introduction

Welcome to Burnout Prevention: A Workbook for Embracing Intentionality and Overcoming Toxic Productivity. In a world where success is frequently equated with constant activity and extended work hours, this workbook provides a refuge for those seeking a more purposeful and sustainable approach to productivity. Within these pages, we challenge the prevailing myths of the modern workplace and encourage you to discover a different path—one that prioritizes well-being, fulfillment, and intentional action over the relentless pursuit of more.

Redefining Productivity: Burnout Prevention

Redefining productivity means shifting our focus from quantity to quality. It's about accomplishing our goals in a way that enriches our lives, not detracts from them. This perspective emphasizes outcomes over output, and well-being over workload. Here, we explore how to set intentions that align with your values and goals, leading to a more purposeful and fulfilling approach to work and life. By prioritizing what truly matters, you can achieve greater satisfaction without sacrificing your health and happiness on the altar of productivity.

HOW TO USE THIS WORKBOOK:

Redefining productivity is about shifting our focus from sheer quantity to meaningful quality—about accomplishing our goals in ways that enrich our lives rather than deplete them. This perspective encourages us to prioritize outcomes over output, well-being over workload. Instead of measuring success solely by how much we do, we measure it by how well we do what truly matters.

Authentic leadership plays a crucial role in this transformation. Leaders who embrace authenticity are grounded in their values, lead with transparency, and encourage others to do the same. They inspire an environment where individuals can pursue their goals in alignment with their deepest values, fostering a sense of purpose and fulfillment. Authentic leadership encourages introspection and intentional action, ensuring that the work we do aligns with our broader life objectives, enriching both our professional and personal lives.

A powerful tool in this process is the Bundy Model, which offers a simple yet effective framework for redefining productivity: Control, Alt, Delete, and Reset. This model is a practical approach to regaining balance and focus in an overstimulated world.

- **Control:** In the face of overwhelming tasks, take control by focusing on what truly matters. Identify priorities that align with your values and ensure your energy goes toward those endeavors, avoiding distractions that lead to burnout.
- **Alt:** This represents a shift in perspective, encouraging you to change your approach when current methods aren't serving you. By rethinking the way you work, you can redefine productivity to emphasize quality over sheer output.
- **Delete:** Let go of what no longer serves you. This could mean eliminating unnecessary tasks, setting boundaries, or even stepping away from obligations that detract from your well-being. Deleting the excess allows space for what truly brings value to your life.
- **Reset:** Regularly take time to reset and reflect. This is about recalibrating your intentions and aligning them with your long-term goals. Resetting allows for a fresh start, ensuring you stay on track with your values and priorities.

Together, these elements of the Bundy Model enable you to shift your mindset from being overwhelmed by productivity to creating a sustainable and fulfilling approach to work and life. By setting clear intentions and aligning them with what matters most, you can find greater satisfaction and success—without sacrificing your health, happiness, or authenticity in the process.

Approach this workbook with an open mind and a willingness to embrace change. By the end, you'll not only have developed a healthier relationship with productivity, but also designed a lifestyle that values quality, purpose, and intentionality above all else. Welcome to your journey beyond busy—where true success is measured by the impact and fulfillment you create, not just the tasks you complete.

RECOGNIZING TOXIC PRODUCTIVITY

- RECOGNIZE THE WARNING SIGNS: UNDERSTAND HOW TOXIC PRODUCTIVITY SHOWS UP IN YOUR DAILY HABITS, SUCH AS GUILT WHEN RESTING, CONSTANT OVER-SCHEDULING, OR MEASURING SELF-WORTH BY OUTPUT, AND HOW THESE BEHAVIORS CAN HARM YOUR MENTAL, EMOTIONAL, AND PHYSICAL WELL-BEING.
- EXPLORE THE IMPACT: EXAMINE HOW THE PRESSURE TO ALWAYS "DO MORE" CAN LEAD TO BURNOUT, REDUCED CREATIVITY, AND DISCONNECTION FROM MEANINGFUL GOALS, ULTIMATELY LOWERING BOTH PERSONAL SATISFACTION AND PROFESSIONAL EFFECTIVENESS.
- APPLY THE BUNDY MODEL: USE THE CONTROL, ALT, DELETE, AND RESET FRAMEWORK TO PAUSE, RE-EVALUATE YOUR HABITS, RELEASE HARMFUL PATTERNS, AND INTENTIONALLY RESET YOUR MINDSET TOWARD HEALTHY, SUSTAINABLE PRODUCTIVITY.

CH.1

Chapter 1: Recognizing Toxic Productivity

In our pursuit of productivity, it's easy to fall into the trap of toxic productivity—the belief that we must always be doing something productive, or else we're wasting time. This chapter will help you recognize the signs of toxic productivity, understand its negative impact on both your well-being and performance, and guide you in identifying your own patterns of overwork.
Using the Bundy Model—Control, Alt, Delete, and Reset—you'll learn practical strategies for breaking free from the cycle of toxic productivity.

Signs and Symptoms of Toxic Productivity

Toxic productivity manifests in various ways, but at its core, it is characterized by an obsession with productivity to the point where it negatively impacts your mental, emotional, and even physical health. Here are some response options applying the Bundy Model:

- Control: Take control of your time and energy by recognizing when you're falling into the trap of constant busyness. Focus on the tasks that truly matter and align with your values.
- Alt: Shift your perspective by rethinking your approach to work. Instead of chasing endless tasks, redefine productivity to prioritize quality and intentionality over quantity.
- Delete: Let go of the unimportant tasks or habits that contribute to burnout and stress. Eliminate distractions that feed into toxic productivity, making space for what truly adds value to your life.
- Reset: Regularly reset your intentions and mindset. Reflect on what's working and what's not, and make adjustments that allow you to operate with purpose and balance.

The Impact on Well-being and Performance

The irony of toxic productivity is that, despite its promise of increased efficiency and success, it often leads to the opposite. The constant pressure to perform can result in:

- **Burnout:** Exhaustion from constant stress and overwork, making it harder to be productive at all.

- **Decreased quality of work:** Rushing through tasks or multitasking can lead to mistakes and lower-quality outcomes.

- **Health issues:** Chronic stress can lead to serious health problems, including heart disease, anxiety disorders, and depression.

- **Strained relationships:** Neglecting personal relationships can lead to isolation and loneliness, further impacting your well-being.

REFLECTION

Identifying Toxic Productivity Patterns

To begin addressing toxic productivity, it's crucial to identify your specific patterns. Reflect on the following questions, and consider writing down your answers in a journal or this workbook:

By understanding toxic productivity and applying the Bundy Model, you'll start to break free from its grip and build a more balanced, purposeful approach to work and life.

When do I feel the need to be most productive, and why?

Consider the times of day, situations, or emotions that trigger a drive for productivity.

What activities do I consider 'productive,' and are these views realistic?

Reflect on whether your standards for productivity are attainable or if they need adjustment.

How do I feel when I'm not being 'productive'?

Explore the emotions associated with downtime or leisure activities. Is there guilt, anxiety, or relief?

What are my physical and emotional responses to my workload?

Note any signs of stress, fatigue, or other health issues related to how you manage your tasks.

How have my relationships been affected by my approach to productivity?

Assess whether your work habits have impacted your connections with others and how.

FOUNDATIONS OF INTENTIONALITY

- LEAD WITH CLARITY AND PURPOSE: DISCOVER HOW ALIGNING DECISIONS WITH CORE VALUES AND LONG-TERM OBJECTIVES HELPS SENIOR LEADERS MAINTAIN FOCUS, INTEGRITY, AND DIRECTION IN HIGH-STAKES ENVIRONMENTS.
- BRIDGE PERSONAL AND PROFESSIONAL VALUES: EXPLORE THE IMPORTANCE OF CONGRUENCE BETWEEN PERSONAL BELIEFS AND LEADERSHIP ACTIONS TO BUILD AUTHENTIC INFLUENCE AND TRUST ACROSS TEAMS.
- ELEVATE STRATEGIC DECISION-MAKING: LEARN HOW INTENTIONALITY TRANSFORMS REACTIVE LEADERSHIP INTO PROACTIVE, VALUE-DRIVEN DECISION-MAKING THAT SUPPORTS SUSTAINABLE GROWTH AND ORGANIZATIONAL ALIGNMENT.

CH.2

Chapter 2: Foundations of Intentionality

Intentionality is the practice of making deliberate decisions that align with your core values, strategic objectives, and what truly matters to you. For senior-level executives, this approach is crucial in leading with purpose and ensuring that both personal and professional actions are driven by a clear sense of direction.

What It Means to Live and Work Intentionally

Living and working intentionally means being deliberate about how you spend your time and energy. It's about choosing activities that not only lead to productivity but also fulfillment and happiness. Intentionality involves:

- **Mindfulness:** Being fully present and aware in each moment, recognizing the impact of your actions.
- **Purpose:** Understanding why you do what you do and ensuring it aligns with your broader life goals.
- **Choice:** Making decisions based on what is most important to you, rather than reacting to external demands.

This chapter will delve into the concept of living and working with intentionality, exploring how to align your daily actions with your long-term values and goals. We will guide you through the process of crafting a personal intention statement—an essential tool that will act as a compass, helping you navigate the complexities of leadership while staying focused on meaningful, high-impact productivity. By applying these principles, you will cultivate a more purposeful approach to decision-making and leadership, ultimately enhancing both your performance and overall fulfillment.

Aligning Actions with Values and Goals

To live intentionally, your actions must reflect your core values and long-term goals. This alignment ensures that your daily efforts contribute to your overall sense of purpose and satisfaction. Here's how to start:

IDENTIFY YOUR CORE VALUES

Reflect on what values are most important to you (e.g., family, health, creativity, integrity). These should guide your decisions and actions.

SET CLEAR GOALS

The exercises are practical steps for applying the concepts discussed. They are your tools for building a foundation of intentional habits.

EVALUATE YOUR CURRENT ACTIVITIES

Assess how your current tasks and projects align with your values and goals. Identify any discrepancies where your time and energy may not be used effectively.

MAKE ADJUSTMENTS

Begin to make conscious choices to spend more time on activities that align with your values and move you towards your goals, and less time on those that don't.

IMPLEMENTATION

Crafting Your Personal Intention Statement

A personal intention statement is a powerful tool to remind you of your core values and goals, guiding your daily actions and decisions. Here's how to create yours:

Reflect on Your Values and Goals

Based on the earlier steps, pinpoint the values and goals that are most important to you.

Envision Your Ideal State

Imagine how you would be living and working if you fully embodied these values and achieved these goals. What does this look like on a daily basis?

Draft Your Statement

Combine your values, goals, and vision of your ideal state into a concise, empowering statement. This should encapsulate what you strive to live by every day.

For example, your intention statement might be, "I choose to approach each day with mindfulness and creativity, focusing on projects that enhance my well-being and contribute to my community, aligning my actions with my commitment to lifelong learning and meaningful connections."

Remember, your intention statement is not set in stone. As you grow and evolve, so too should your statement. Revisit and revise it as necessary to reflect your current values and goals.

DECLUTTERING YOUR MIND AND SPACE

- MENTAL CLARITY BEGINS WITH LETTING GO: EXPLORE HOW RELEASING NEGATIVE THOUGHTS, LIMITING BELIEFS, AND MENTAL OVERLOAD CREATES SPACE FOR FOCUS, CREATIVITY, AND EMOTIONAL BALANCE.
- THE POWER OF PHYSICAL ENVIRONMENT: UNDERSTAND HOW AN ORGANIZED, CLUTTER-FREE SPACE CAN REDUCE STRESS, BOOST PRODUCTIVITY, AND REFLECT A CLEAR, INTENTIONAL MINDSET.
- ALIGN YOUR INNER AND OUTER WORLDS: LEARN PRACTICAL STRATEGIES TO DECLUTTER BOTH MENTALLY AND PHYSICALLY, CREATING HARMONY BETWEEN YOUR ENVIRONMENT AND YOUR EMOTIONAL WELL-BEING.

CH.3

Chapter 3: Decluttering Your Mind and Space

Decluttering isn't just about organizing your physical surroundings; it's also about clearing your mind of unnecessary clutter that hampers productivity and well-being. This chapter delves into strategies for reducing mental clutter and creating a workspace that reflects intentionality, followed by a structured exercise to help you develop your own decluttering action plan.

Mindful Techniques to Reduce Mental Clutter

Mental clutter can take many forms, from lingering worries about the future to a mental to-do list that seems ever-expanding. Reducing this clutter is crucial for achieving clarity, focus, and peace. Here are some techniques:

MINDFULNESS MEDITATION

Practice sitting quietly for a few minutes each day, focusing on your breath. When your mind wanders, gently bring your attention back. This can help you become more aware of mental clutter without getting overwhelmed by it.

JOURNALING

Writing down your thoughts, worries, and tasks can transfer them from your mind to paper, helping to clear your mental space.

SET CLEAR PRIORITIES

Define what's most important to accomplish each day. Focusing on a few key priorities can help reduce the feeling of being overwhelmed by tasks.

DIGITAL DETOX

Set aside specific times to disconnect from electronic devices. This can help reduce information overload and give your mind a break. Rule of thumb: 80% Teaching and 20% fun videos (it's good to laugh). Time is priceless so use it to grow.

Creating a Purposeful Workspace

Your physical environment plays a significant role in your productivity and state of mind. An intentional workspace is one that promotes focus, creativity, and tranquility:

- **Eliminate Clutter:** Start by removing items that are not essential to your work. A clear space can lead to a clear mind.
- **Organize Thoughtfully:** Arrange your remaining items in a way that makes sense for your workflow. Consider ergonomic setups for comfort and efficiency.

- **Incorporate Personal Touches:** Add elements that inspire you or make you happy, such as plants, artwork, or personal mementos. These should enhance your space without causing distraction.
- **Consider Lighting and Comfort:** Good lighting can reduce eye strain and boost your mood. Ensure your chair and desk are comfortable and support a healthy posture.

EXERCISE

Intentional Decluttering Action Plan

A personal intention statement is a powerful tool to remind you of your core values and goals, guiding your daily actions and decisions. Here's how to create yours:

Assessment

Spend a day observing the sources of clutter in your mind and workspace. Note what disrupts your focus or contributes to feelings of overwhelm.

Prioritization

Decide which areas need the most attention. Is it your digital clutter, your physical workspace, or specific mental worries?

Action Steps

For each area identified, list specific, actionable steps to declutter. This might include setting aside time for a digital detox, scheduling daily journaling, or organizing your desk.

Implementation

Choose one action step to implement this week. Schedule it as you would any important appointment.

Reflection and Adjustment

At the end of the week, reflect on the impact of this action. Did it reduce clutter? How did it affect your productivity and well-being? Adjust your plan based on what you learn and tackle the next priority.

This exercise is not a one-time event but a process of continual improvement. Over time, you'll develop habits that help keep both your mind and workspace clear and purposeful.

PRIORITIZING YOUR WELL-BEING

- REDEFINE PRODUCTIVITY THROUGH WELL-BEING: UNDERSTAND HOW TRUE PRODUCTIVITY IS SUSTAINED BY PRIORITIZING SELF-CARE, NOT CONSTANT OUTPUT, AND HOW NEGLECTING YOUR WELL-BEING DIMINISHES LONG-TERM EFFECTIVENESS.
- PROTECT YOUR ENERGY WITH BOUNDARIES: LEARN HOW TO ESTABLISH AND MAINTAIN HEALTHY BOUNDARIES THAT PREVENT BURNOUT AND PRESERVE MENTAL, EMOTIONAL, AND PHYSICAL ENERGY.
- DESIGN A PERSONALIZED SELF-CARE ROUTINE: USE A GUIDED EXERCISE TO CREATE A SELF-CARE PLAN TAILORED TO YOUR LIFESTYLE AND NEEDS, ENSURING BALANCE, RESILIENCE, AND SUSTAINABLE PRODUCTIVITY.

CH.4

Chapter 4: Prioritizing Your Well-being

Understanding the intrinsic link between your well-being and productivity is crucial. This chapter focuses on the importance of self-care as a foundational element of productive living, how to set healthy boundaries to protect your energy, and provides a structured exercise to help you design a personalized self-care routine.

The Role of Self-care in Productivity

Self-care is often misconceived as a luxury or an afterthought in the pursuit of productivity. However, it's a vital component of sustaining high performance and creativity over the long term. Self-care includes any intentional actions taken to care for your physical, mental, and emotional health, and it has a direct impact on your productivity by:

- **Enhancing Focus:** Regular self-care practices, such as adequate sleep and mindfulness exercises, can improve concentration and mental clarity.
- **Boosting Energy Levels:** Activities that nourish your body, like exercise and healthy eating, provide the energy needed to tackle your tasks.
- **Improving Resilience:** Emotional and psychological self-care, such as social connections and hobbies, help buffer against stress and burnout.

Setting Healthy Boundaries

Setting boundaries is an essential aspect of self-care. It involves knowing your limits and communicating them clearly to others. Healthy boundaries can include:

- **Work-Life Balance:** Defining clear times when you are working and when you are off, ensuring you have time for rest and activities that bring you joy.
- **Saying No:** Feeling empowered to decline additional responsibilities or engagements that would compromise your well-being.
- **Digital Detox:** Setting limits on screen time to reduce information overload and increase quality time with yourself and loved ones.

EXERCISE

Creating Your Mindful Weekly Planner

This exercise will help you apply mindful planning and time management strategies to your own life, creating a balanced and intentional weekly schedule.

Reflect on Your Priorities

Write down your key priorities for the week, both personal and professional. Consider what tasks or activities are essential to moving you towards your goals.

Assign Time Blocks

Using a weekly planner, assign time blocks for your essential tasks. Ensure to include blocks for self-care, exercise, and leisure to maintain balance.

Plan for Flexibility

Leave some blocks of time open for unexpected tasks or to give yourself a buffer. This helps reduce stress when things don't go as planned.

Review and Adjust

At the end of the week, review your planner. Reflect on what went well and what didn't. Were you realistic in your planning? Did you allocate enough time for self-care and leisure? Adjust your planning for the next week based on your reflections.

Mindful Weekly Planner Template

WEEKLY INTENTIONS

PERSONAL GOAL:

PROFESSIONAL GOAL:

SELF-CARE GOAL:

PRIORITIES THIS WEEK

MUST-DO TASKS (PROFESSIONAL):

MUST-DO TASKS (PERSONAL):

SELF-CARE ACTIVITIES:

TIME BLOCKING SCHEDULE

Time Block	Mon	Tue	Wed	Thu	Fri	Sat	Sun
6am - 9am							
9am - 12pm							
12pm - 3pm							
3pm - 6pm							
6pm - 9pm							
9pm - 11pm							

DAILY REFLECTIONS

WHAT WENT WELL?

WHAT COULD BE IMPROVED?

BALANCE DRIVES SUCCESS

- CONNECT WELL-BEING TO CAREER SUCCESS: EXPLORE HOW YOUR MENTAL, EMOTIONAL, AND PHYSICAL HEALTH DIRECTLY IMPACT YOUR PROFESSIONAL GROWTH, CLARITY, AND CONFIDENCE IN YOUR DAILY WORK.
- OWN YOUR WORKDAY WITH CONFIDENCE: LEARN HOW ORGANIZING TASKS WITHIN A SET TIMEFRAME AND BEING PROUD OF WHAT YOU ACCOMPLISH CAN REDUCE STRESS, PREVENT OVERWORKING, AND BOOST JOB SATISFACTION.
- BUILD A BOUNDARIED, CAREER-FOCUSED ROUTINE: USE A STRUCTURED APPROACH TO CREATE A SUSTAINABLE WORK RHYTHM THAT HONORS BOTH YOUR AMBITION AND YOUR NEED FOR REST, FOCUS, AND PERSONAL TIME.

CH.5

Chapter 5: Balance Drives Success

Understanding the intrinsic link between your well-being and career is crucial. This chapter focuses on the importance of organizing work and being confident in what was accomplished during your scheduled work timeframe. As a foundational element of productive working, how to set healthy boundaries to protect your energy and provide a structured organizational routine to help you design a healthy career-focused routine.

In a world where busyness is often mistaken for success, the intersection of well-being and career growth is more important than ever. Too often, professionals sacrifice their mental, emotional, and physical health for the sake of perceived productivity, only to find themselves overwhelmed, exhausted, and uninspired. True success isn't just measured by what you accomplish, it is also about how you feel while achieving it.
Connect Well-Being to Career Success

Your health is not separate from your ambition. It fuels it. Mental clarity enhances decision-making, emotional stability strengthens leadership, and physical wellness supports endurance. When you are balanced internally, you're more likely to approach challenges creatively, communicate clearly, and perform consistently.

Stress, burnout, and chronic fatigue are not badges of honor. They are warning signs that your professional pace is out of sync with your personal capacity. Reclaiming this balance begins with self-awareness. How do you feel at the start of your workday? Do you wake up energized or already behind? Reflecting on your well-being allows you to realign your habits to support long-term growth.

Own Your Workday with Confidence

One of the most empowering shifts you can make is moving from reacting to your day to actively owning it. Organizing tasks within a realistic timeframe, then acknowledging what you've accomplished, even if it wasn't everything, builds confidence and reduces unnecessary stress.
Start with time-blocking. Prioritize your top three goals each day and set clear boundaries around work time and rest time. Avoid the trap of believing that staying busy equals being productive. What matters most is focused, meaningful work followed by intentional rest.
Celebrate small wins. Instead of focusing on what's left undone, acknowledge the progress you have made. This mindset shift nurtures confidence and boosts your sense of control, even on challenging days.

Build a Boundaried, Career-Focused Routine

Productivity without boundaries is a fast track to burnout. Creating a structured work routine doesn't just make you more efficient—it preserves your energy and protects your peace. A career-focused routine should support your goals and your well-being.
Here's a simple framework to build your routine:

- Morning Grounding: Begin with 10–15 minutes of centering—whether it's meditation, journaling, or stretching. This grounds your mind before work begins.
- Work Blocks: Schedule focused work sessions (90-minute blocks with 15-minute breaks) to optimize productivity and attention.

- Clear Cutoffs: Establish a set time to end your workday. Communicate this boundary and respect it yourself.
- Reflection & Planning: Take 10 minutes at the end of each day to note accomplishments, reflect on challenges, and plan for tomorrow.

Don't forget: Rest is part of the routine. Protect your off-time as fiercely as you do your meetings. Whether it is exercise, reading, family time, or solitude, non-work time replenishes the drive you need to lead effectively.

Reflection Questions:

- How does your current work routine support or hinder your well-being?
- What are three ways you can protect your energy during your workday?
- When was the last time you celebrated what you accomplished instead of focusing on what you didn't?

BUILDING RESILIENCE AGAINST DISTRACTIONS

- IDENTIFY AND OVERCOME DISTRACTIONS: LEARN TO RECOGNIZE BOTH INTERNAL AND EXTERNAL DISTRACTIONS THAT INTERRUPT YOUR WORKFLOW AND UNDERSTAND THE EMOTIONAL TRIGGERS BEHIND THEM.
- CULTIVATE DEEP WORK HABITS: DISCOVER PRACTICAL ROUTINES AND TECHNIQUES SUCH AS TIME-BLOCKING, ENVIRONMENT DESIGN, AND DIGITAL BOUNDARIES THAT SUPPORT SUSTAINED, FOCUSED WORK SESSIONS.
- DEVELOP A DISTRACTION MITIGATION STRATEGY: ENGAGE IN A GUIDED EXERCISE TO TRACK YOUR DISTRACTION PATTERNS AND CREATE A PERSONALIZED PLAN TO STRENGTHEN FOCUS AND IMPROVE PRODUCTIVITY.

CH.6

Chapter 6: Building Resilience Against Distractions

In an age where distractions are only a click away, building resilience against them is crucial for maintaining focus and achieving deep work. This chapter explores strategies for identifying and overcoming distractions, cultivating habits that encourage deep, focused work sessions, and includes an exercise to develop your own distraction mitigation strategy.

Identifying and Overcoming Distractions

The first step in building resilience against distractions is identifying them. Distractions can be external, like phone notifications or interruptions from others, or internal, like wandering thoughts or emotional discomfort. To overcome these distractions:

- **Awareness:** Keep a distraction log for a few days. Note what distracts you and when. Understanding your distraction patterns is key to addressing them.
- **Environment:** Modify your environment to reduce external distractions. This might involve using noise-cancelling headphones, turning off notifications, or creating a designated workspace.
- **Mindset:** Address internal distractions by practicing mindfulness or meditation to improve your ability to refocus your attention. Techniques like the Pomodoro Technique can also help train your focus.

Cultivating Deep Work Habits

Deep work refers to the ability to focus without distraction on cognitively demanding tasks. Cultivating habits that encourage deep work involves:

- **Scheduled Deep Work Sessions:** Allocate specific times in your day or week for uninterrupted work on high-priority tasks. Treat these blocks as non-negotiable appointments with yourself.
- **Rituals:** Create a start-up ritual to signal to your brain that it's time for deep work. This could be as simple as a cup of tea, a few minutes of stretching, or reviewing your goals for the session.
- **Limit Multitasking:** Focus on one task at a time. Multitasking can make it difficult to enter a state of deep work and significantly reduces the quality of your output.
- **Rest:** Incorporate regular breaks and downtime into your schedule. Rest is not the opposite of productivity; it's an essential component of sustained deep work.

In an age where attention is one of our most valuable currencies, protecting it is both a challenge and a necessity. With every ping, notification, and scrolling opportunity, our brains are pulled away from meaningful work and toward fleeting stimulation. Over time, this digital noise erodes our focus, fractures our productivity, and compromises our ability to engage in what author Cal Newport calls “deep work,” the kind of work that produces real value, insight, and progress.
If you have ever ended the day feeling exhausted but unsure of what you accomplished, you’re not alone. Distractions don’t just steal your time. They chip away at your momentum, confidence, and creative energy. The good news? Focus is a skill, and like any skill, it can be trained.

Recognize the Roots of Distraction
Distractions aren’t just external. They often reflect something internal. Boredom, fear of failure, perfectionism, or even stress can make our minds crave quick dopamine hits from checking our phones, multitasking, or clicking between tabs. The first step in building distraction resilience is becoming honest about why you’re avoiding focused work.

Ask yourself:
- What tasks do I avoid, and why?
- What emotions come up when I try to focus?
- What are my top three digital distractions?

Understanding the emotional triggers behind distraction empowers you to respond with intention rather than reaction.

Create a Deep Work Ritual
Deep work doesn’t just happen—it requires intention, structure, and repetition. Developing a personal ritual helps signal your brain that it’s time to focus and supports you in creating a flow state.
Try this Deep Work Routine:
1. Designate a Work Zone: Choose a physical or digital space free of unnecessary noise and clutter.
2. Set a Clear Goal: Before each session, define what you want to accomplish.
3. Time-Block Your Session: Work in focused intervals—try the Pomodoro Technique (25 minutes work / 5 minutes rest) or deep-focus blocks (90 minutes of uninterrupted work).
4. Silence Digital Intrusions: Turn off non-essential notifications. Use apps or browser extensions like Freedom or Cold Turkey to block tempting sites.
5. Decompress: End each session with a 5-minute review—acknowledge what you achieved, and identify where you lost focus and why.

Build Habits That Support Focus
Sustainable focus is less about willpower and more about environment, habits, and clarity. Here are three powerful habits to strengthen your attention muscle:
- **Start with Stillness:** Begin your day without screens. A few moments of silence, journaling, or breathwork primes your brain for focused thinking.
- **Batch Similar Tasks:** Grouping similar tasks (like emails or calls) reduces the cognitive cost of switching between different types of work.
- **Schedule Distraction Time:** Paradoxically, giving yourself permission to check social media or browse freely but on a schedule can reduce the impulse to do it constantly.

Exercise: Build Your Distraction Mitigation Strategy

Use this simple framework to create a personalized strategy that builds awareness and resilience.

Trigger	Distraction Type	Underlying Emotion	Prevention Strategy
Example: Afternoon fatigue	Instagram scrolling	Boredom, burnout	Take a 10-minute walk, switch to a lighter task

Instructions:

1. Track your distractions for three days.
2. Fill out at least three common patterns in the table.
3. Choose one strategy to implement this week and reflect on its impact.

Reflection Questions:

- When am I most vulnerable to distractions during my day?
- What tasks or goals do I avoid, and what's really driving that avoidance?
- How can I create an environment that honors my need for focus?

EXERCISE

Create A Distraction Log and Develop Your Mitigation Strategy

DISTRACTION LOG EXAMPLE

Goals	Date	Time	Distraction	Source (External/ Internal)	Duration	Impact on Work (Low/ Medium/ High)	Possible Counter-measures
Avoid media Distraction	03-14	10:00 AM	Social media notification	External	5 mins	Medium	Turn off notifications during work
Focus on Work	03-14	11:30 AM	Worrying about personal issues	Internal	20 mins	High	Schedule a specific time to address personal concerns
Avoid Over-Socializing	03-14	2:00 PM	Co-workers stopping by to chat	External	15 mins	Low	Set specific times for socializing
	...	...	...	...	...	...	...

How to Use A Distraction Log

- **Fill in the Log:** Throughout your day, whenever you find yourself distracted from a task, note it in the log. Be as specific as possible about the nature of the distraction, its source, and how long it diverted your attention from your work.
- **Assess the Impact:** Evaluate how significantly each distraction impacted your work. This will help you prioritize which distractions to address first based on their effect on your productivity.
- **Identify Patterns:** After logging distractions for a week or more, review your log to identify patterns. Are there specific times of day when you're more prone to certain types of distractions? Do external interruptions dominate, or are internal distractions more disruptive?
- **Plan Countermeasures:** For each recurring distraction, brainstorm possible ways to reduce or eliminate it. These might include environmental changes, schedule adjustments, or mindfulness techniques for internal distractions.
- **Implement and Review:** Start implementing the countermeasures you've identified, focusing on the most disruptive distractions first. Periodically review your log and the effectiveness of your strategies, making adjustments as needed.

EXERCISE

Create A Distraction Log and Develop Your Mitigation Strategy

DISTRACTION LOG TEMPLATE

Goals	Date	Time	Distraction	Source (External/ Internal)	Duration	Impact on Work (Low/ Medium/ High)	Possible Counter-measures
	...	...	...	...	...	...	...

How to Use A Distraction Log

- **Fill in the Log:** Throughout your day, whenever you find yourself distracted from a task, note it in the log. Be as specific as possible about the nature of the distraction, its source, and how long it diverted your attention from your work.
- **Assess the Impact:** Evaluate how significantly each distraction impacted your work. This will help you prioritize which distractions to address first based on their effect on your productivity.
- **Identify Patterns:** After logging distractions for a week or more, review your log to identify patterns. Are there specific times of day when you're more prone to certain types of distractions? Do external interruptions dominate, or are internal distractions more disruptive?
- **Plan Countermeasures:** For each recurring distraction, brainstorm possible ways to reduce or eliminate it. These might include environmental changes, schedule adjustments, or mindfulness techniques for internal distractions.
- **Implement and Review:** Start implementing the countermeasures you've identified, focusing on the most disruptive distractions first. Periodically review your log and the effectiveness of your strategies, making adjustments as needed.

THE POWER OF SAYING “NO”

- ALIGN DECISIONS WITH PURPOSE: UNDERSTAND HOW SAYING NO TO MISALIGNED REQUESTS PROTECTS YOUR TIME, ENERGY, AND VALUES, ALLOWING YOU TO FOCUS ON WHAT TRULY MATTERS.
- OVERCOME GUILT AND PRESSURE: EXPLORE THE EMOTIONAL CHALLENGES OF DECLINING OTHERS AND LEARN STRATEGIES TO SAY NO WITH CONFIDENCE AND CLARITY.
- PRACTICE INTENTIONAL REFUSAL: USE A GUIDED EXERCISE TO BUILD YOUR "NO" MUSCLE, HELPING YOU CREATE HEALTHY BOUNDARIES AND REINFORCE INTENTIONAL, VALUE-DRIVEN LIVING.

CH.7

Chapter 7: The Power of Saying "No"

Mastering the art of saying no is a critical skill in the journey toward intentional living and productivity. This chapter explores the significance of declining requests that don't align with your values or priorities, the importance of focusing on what truly matters, and provides an exercise to practice intentional refusal.

Learning to Decline with Intention

Saying no is often challenging, particularly in a culture that prizes busyness and overcommitment. However, learning to decline requests with intention is vital for preserving your time, energy, and focus for the things that are genuinely important. To decline with intention:

- **Understand Your Priorities:** Be clear on your values and goals. This clarity makes it easier to assess whether a request aligns with your priorities.
- **Communicate Clearly and Respectfully:** When saying no, be direct but polite. Offer a brief explanation if appropriate, but remember that you are not obligated to justify your decision.
- **Practice Self-compassion:** Recognize that you have limited time and energy. Saying no is a form of self-care and not a sign of failure or weakness.

The Importance of Focusing on What Truly Matters

Every time you say yes to something that is not aligned with your values or priorities, you are effectively saying no to something that is. Focusing on what truly matters means making conscious choices about where to invest your finite resources. This focus enables you to:

- **Enhance Your Well-being:** By prioritizing activities that align with your values and goals, you contribute to your own mental, emotional, and physical well-being.
- **Improve Your Performance:** Concentrating on fewer, more meaningful tasks can lead to higher quality work and greater satisfaction.
- **Build Stronger Relationships:** Investing time and energy in relationships that are important to you becomes more feasible when you're not overcommitted.

In a culture that often glorifies busyness and self-sacrifice, saying "yes" can feel like the default response. Yes to helping others, yes to one more task, yes to expectations that don't belong to us. But every "yes" we offer without intention is a quiet "no" to our priorities, energy, and well-being.

Mastering the art of saying no is not about being selfish—it's about being strategic. It's about creating space for what truly matters and protecting your capacity to show up fully where you're most needed.

Why Saying No Matters?
Your time, attention, and energy are finite. When you spend them on things that don't align with your values or goals, you dilute your impact and increase the risk of burnout. Every time you agree to something that doesn't serve you, you're pulling resources away from the things that do.

Intentional refusal is a declaration of purpose. It is a powerful boundary that affirms your clarity, preserves your focus, and reinforces that you are in control of your commitments, not the other way around.

The Emotional Challenge of No
Many people struggle with saying no because they fear disappointing others, appearing unhelpful, or damaging relationships. These feelings are valid, but they shouldn't control your decisions.

When you say no with honesty and respect, you build trust with yourself and others. People may not always like your answer, but they will respect your integrity when you communicate clearly and compassionately.

Here are a few helpful reframes:
- Saying no is not rejection—it's redirection.
- Declining one request doesn't mean you're unkind—it means you're aware of your limits.
- Every no creates space for a more meaningful yes.

Clarity First, Then Refusal
Before you can confidently say no, you must first be clear on your priorities. Take a moment to reflect:
- What are your top 3 priorities this season?
- What are your non-negotiables?
- Where do you most want to invest your time and energy?

When your values are clear, your boundaries become easier to define—and easier to defend.

The Confident No: A Practice
Saying no doesn't need to be harsh or abrupt. It can be direct, kind, and firm. Practice these respectful ways to decline:
- "Thank you for thinking of me, but I can't commit to that right now."
- "That sounds like a great opportunity, but it doesn't align with my focus at this time."
- "I appreciate the invite, but I need to prioritize other responsibilities."

The more often you practice, the more natural it will become.

Exercise: Practicing Intentional Refusal

Use this simple framework to reflect on recent or upcoming decisions:

Request or Obligation	Does It Align With My Priorities?	Emotional Response	My Response Strategy
Example: Volunteering for an extra work project	No	Guilt, pressure to say yes	Politely decline and suggest another resource or timeline

Instructions:

1. Identify 2–3 situations where you feel pressured to say yes.
2. Fill out the table to examine each situation.
3. Draft and practice your response in advance.

Reflection Questions:

- What are the fears or emotions that surface when I say no?
- When was the last time I said yes to something I didn't truly want to do?
- How can I create more space for my priorities by learning to say no more often?

Saying no is a courageous act of self-respect. It's not about shutting people out—it's about showing up fully where you're meant to be. When you protect your time and energy, you not only become more productive, you become more present, more focused, and more aligned with the life and work you truly desire.

EXERCISE

Practicing Intentional Refusal

Developing the skill of saying no takes practice. This exercise is designed to help you become more comfortable with intentional refusal:

Reflect on Recent Requests

Think about the last few requests or commitments you agreed to. Were they in line with your priorities? How did saying yes make you feel?

Identify a Request to Decline

Consider upcoming or recurring requests that you typically agree to out of obligation, not desire or necessity. Choose one that you will decline next time it arises.

Plan Your Response

Craft a polite but firm response. Practice saying it out loud or writing it down. Remember, being respectful does not mean you have to provide a lengthy justification.

Commit to Saying No

When the opportunity arises, use your planned response to decline the request. Observe how it feels to assert your boundaries and prioritize your needs.

Reflect on the Experience

Afterward, reflect on the experience. How did the person respond? How did saying no affect your stress levels, your time, or your ability to focus on your priorities?

Through regular practice, saying no will become less daunting and more empowering. It's a crucial step in reclaiming your time and living more intentionally, allowing you to dedicate yourself fully to the pursuits that matter most.

CULTIVATING PRODUCTIVE HABITS

- ALIGN HABITS WITH INTENTIONS: LEARN HOW TO BUILD DAILY HABITS THAT REFLECT YOUR VALUES AND LONG-TERM GOALS, RATHER THAN SOCIETAL PRESSURE OR UNREALISTIC PRODUCTIVITY STANDARDS.
- LEVERAGE ROUTINE FOR SUSTAINABLE GROWTH: EXPLORE HOW INTENTIONAL ROUTINES CREATE STRUCTURE, REDUCE DECISION FATIGUE, AND SUPPORT A HEALTHY, BALANCED APPROACH TO PRODUCTIVITY.
- CREATE YOUR INTENTIONAL HABITS PLAN: ENGAGE IN A GUIDED EXERCISE TO DESIGN A PERSONALIZED ROUTINE THAT PROMOTES FOCUS, WELL-BEING, AND MEANINGFUL PROGRESS TOWARD YOUR GOALS.

CH.8

Chapter 8: Cultivating Productive Habits

Developing habits that support your intentions and goals is fundamental to overcoming toxic productivity and fostering a genuinely productive lifestyle. This chapter delves into how to form habits that align with intentional living, examines the role of routine in promoting healthy productivity, and includes an exercise for creating your intentional habits plan.

Forming Habits that Align with Intentional Living

Intentional living requires habits that reflect your values and aspirations. To form such habits:

- **Start Small:** Choose one small habit you'd like to develop that aligns with your values and goals. Something manageable increases the likelihood of consistency.
- **Understand Your Why:** Clearly articulate why this habit is important to you and how it connects to your larger goals. This understanding will help motivate you when you're struggling to stick with it.
- **Create Triggers:** Link your new habit to an established routine or specific cue, making it easier to remember and perform the new behavior.
- **Be Patient and Persistent:** Forming a new habit takes time and effort. Be patient with yourself and persistent in your efforts, even when you encounter setbacks.

The Role of Routine in Combating Toxic Productivity

A well-structured routine can be a powerful tool against toxic productivity. Routines can:

- **Provide Structure:** Knowing what to expect each day can reduce anxiety and decision fatigue, making it easier to focus on what's important.
- **Ensure Balance:** Incorporating breaks, leisure, and self-care into your routine ensures a healthier balance between work and rest.
- **Promote Focus:** Dedicated time blocks for deep work help minimize distractions, allowing for more focused and effective task completion.

Creating Your Intentional Habits Plan

Use the following steps to build a routine rooted in intentional living:

Step 1: Define Your Priorities
Identify the top 3 areas you want to focus on right now (e.g., self-care, creativity, leadership, wellness).

Step 2: Choose Supportive Habits
List 1–2 habits that support each priority. Make sure they are specific and actionable.

Priority	Habit	When/How Often
Self-care	Morning journaling	Daily, 10 minutes after waking up
Creativity	30 minutes of distraction-free writing	Tuesdays and Thursdays, 6–6:30 PM
Wellness	Evening walk	Every other day after dinner

Step 3: Make It Visible
Use a habit tracker, planner, or phone reminder to help reinforce consistency and accountability.

Step 4: Reflect and Adjust Weekly
At the end of each week, ask:

- What worked well?
- What felt forced or draining?
- What needs to be adjusted to better support my intention?

Reflection Questions:

- What habits have I developed out of pressure rather than purpose?
- How can I make my routine a reflection of what I truly value?
- What is one small habit I can start today that supports intentional productivity?

You don't need to do more, you need to do what matters most. When your habits reflect your values, productivity becomes purposeful, your energy becomes sacred, and your success becomes sustainable. Building habits with intention isn't just a strategy, it's a lifestyle shift.

EXERCISE

Developing Your Intentional Habits Plan

Creating a plan for developing and integrating new habits into your life can help transform your intentions into action. Follow these steps:

Identify Habits to Cultivate

Based on your goals and values, list habits that you believe will support your intentional living. Select one to start with, following the principle of starting small.

Define Your Why

For the habit you've chosen, write down why it's important to you and how it supports your larger goals. This will serve as your motivation.

Plan for Implementation

Determine how you will integrate this habit into your daily routine. What time of day will you perform it? What trigger will remind you to do it? How will you track your progress?

Prepare for Challenges

Think about potential obstacles to maintaining your new habit and plan for how to address them. This could include setting reminders, asking for support from friends or family, or adjusting your environment to reduce barriers.

Reflect and Adjust

After a few weeks, reflect on your progress. What's working well? What challenges have you encountered? Adjust your plan as needed to better support your habit formation.

Intentional Habits Plan Template

Habit Identification

Habit to Develop:

What small, manageable habit do you want to start with?

Why It Matters (Define Your Why):

Why is this habit important to you?

How does it align with your broader goals or values?

Implementation Plan

Trigger:

What routine or cue will trigger this habit?

Routine:

When and where will you perform this habit?

How often (daily, three times a week, etc.)?

Reward:

How will you reward yourself for sticking to this habit?

Tracking and Accountability

Progress Tracking:

How will you track your progress (journal, app, calendar)?

Accountability:

Who will you share your progress with for accountability (friend, family, online group)?

Obstacle Planning

Potential Obstacles:

What might hinder your ability to perform this habit?

Solutions:

What strategies can you employ to overcome these obstacles?

Review and Adjustment

Weekly Reflection:

Did you perform the habit as planned?

What successes or challenges did you encounter?

Reward:

Adjustments:

This template is designed to be flexible and can be used for any habit you're looking to cultivate. Regularly reviewing and adjusting your plan is key to making lasting changes. Remember, the goal is progress, not perfection.

INTEGRATING REST, REFLECTION, AND SUSTAINED INTENTIONALITY

- EMBRACE REST AS A STRATEGY: UNDERSTAND THE VITAL ROLE OF REST AND INTENTIONAL DOWNTIME IN SUSTAINING ENERGY, CREATIVITY, AND LONG-TERM PRODUCTIVITY.
- PRIORITIZE ONGOING REFLECTION: EXPLORE HOW REGULAR SELF-ASSESSMENT AND MINDFUL REFLECTION KEEP YOUR HABITS AND GOALS ALIGNED WITH YOUR EVOLVING VALUES AND LIFE CIRCUMSTANCES.
- SUSTAIN AND ADAPT YOUR PRACTICES: LEARN PRACTICAL STRATEGIES TO MAINTAIN MOMENTUM WHILE REMAINING FLEXIBLE, ALLOWING YOUR INTENTIONAL LIVING JOURNEY TO GROW WITH YOU OVER TIME.

CH.9

Chapter 9: The Stillness Strategy: Cultivating Rest, Reflection, and Purposeful Living

As we reach the culmination of our journey towards intentional living and productivity, it becomes essential to integrate the principles of rest and reflection while considering how to sustain this lifestyle over time. This final chapter combines the essence of embracing downtime and ongoing reflection with strategies to maintain momentum and adapt your practices as your life and goals evolve.

The Critical Role of Downtime in Productivity

Contrary to the hustle culture, rest is not the enemy of productivity but its ally. Scheduled downtime plays a crucial role in maintaining long-term productivity by preventing burnout, enhancing creativity, and improving decision-making. Incorporate rest into your routine as deliberately as you do your work, treating it as a non-negotiable component of your success.

Regular Reflection to Enhance Intentionality

Reflection is the process of examining your actions, decisions, and their outcomes to learn and plan better for the future. It enhances intentionality by ensuring that your actions continue to align with your values and goals. Set aside regular times for reflection—daily, weekly, or monthly—to assess your progress, acknowledge your achievements, and identify areas for adjustment.

The Rhythm of Rest

As we arrive at the culmination of this journey toward intentional living and meaningful productivity, there is one final principle that holds it all together: sustainability. In a world that constantly pushes us to strive, hustle, and achieve, it's easy to forget that rest, reflection, and recalibration are not signs of weakness. They are the very foundation of long-term success. True intentional living isn't rigid. It flows. And just as every inhale must be followed by an exhale, every season of momentum requires a rhythm of rest.

Embrace Rest as a Strategy

Rest is not the opposite of productivity, it is what makes it possible. Without rest, even the best systems, habits, and routines eventually unravel. Rest is where ideas settle, energy is restored, and clarity is regained. It's the space where creativity lives and where emotional regulation is strengthened. There are different forms of rest that all play a role in sustainability:

- Physical rest (sleep, stillness, slowing down)
- Mental rest (disconnecting from tasks, reducing stimulation)
- Emotional rest (safe spaces, solitude, releasing pressure to perform)
- Creative rest (pausing consumption to spark original thought)

To lead an intentional life, you must be willing to step back, pause, and let rest become part of your rhythm, not just something you earn, but something you need.

Prioritize Ongoing Reflection

Reflection is the compass that keeps your path aligned with your purpose. It helps you ask the deeper questions:

- Is what I'm doing still aligned with who I'm becoming?
- Have my values shifted? Are my actions keeping pace?
- What do I need more of? What can I let go of?

Make space each week or at least each month for a check-in with yourself. Journal, meditate, or simply sit in silence and take inventory of your energy, goals, and emotions. These moments of reflection ensure that you remain anchored, even as life changes around you.

Reflection Ritual Starter Questions:

- What gave me life this week?
- What drained me?
- What do I want to carry into next week?
- What do I want to leave behind?

EXERCISE

Implementing Rest and Reflective Practices

Schedule Downtime

Identify times in your weekly schedule that you can dedicate to rest. Consider activities that truly rejuvenate you—whether that's reading, walking in nature, or spending time with loved ones.

Reflection Ritual

Establish a regular reflection ritual. Use a journal to document your thoughts, feelings, successes, and areas for growth. Reflect on how closely your actions align with your intentional living goals.

Mindfulness Moments

Incorporate short mindfulness exercises into your day to connect with the present moment, especially during transitions between different activities.

Sustaining Intentional Living

Maintaining the momentum of intentional living requires ongoing effort and the willingness to adapt. Life changes, and so will your priorities and goals. The key to sustained intentionality is remaining flexible and open to modifying your practices as needed.

Adjusting and Evolving Your Practices Over Time

As you grow and your circumstances change, revisit and reassess your values, goals, and the habits that support them. Be prepared to let go of practices that no longer serve you and to embrace new ones that better align with your evolving self.

EXERCISE

Crafting Your Long-Term Intentionality Blueprint

Vision for the Future

Write a detailed vision of what intentional living looks like for you in the coming years. Consider different areas of your life such as career, relationships, health, and personal growth.

Evaluate and Plan

Annually or biannually, evaluate your progress towards this vision. Identify what adjustments are needed in your habits, routines, and priorities to keep you on track.

Support System

Consider who in your life can support your journey towards sustained intentionality. Share your goals and plans with them and discuss how you can mutually support each other.